Paddling the California Coast

River Mouths ~ Lagoons ~ Tidal Estuaries ~ Marshes ~ Bays

A Quiet Water Guide To Paddler's Paradise

John Coale

Changing Sky Publications ~ Cedar Ridge, CA

Readers should pay strict attention to the advisory
statements of each listing in this book and
should consult current information sources to obtain
up-to-date conditions at any of these locations.

Although the author and publisher have exhaustively
researched all sources to ensure the accuracy and
completeness of the information contained in this
book, we assume no responsibility for errors, inaccu-
racies, omissions or any other inconsistency herein.
Any slights against people or organizaitons are
unintentional.

ISBN: 0-9662821-1-6

First Edition Printed 2001
Printed in the United States of America

Produced by Changing Sky Publications
P.O.Box 1390
Cedar Ridge, CA 95924

Acknowledgements

The author would like to express his heartfelt thanks to the following people and organizations for their help and support: **Chalk Bluff Inc** for their beautiful digital relief map, which graces the back cover of this book, the **US Geographical Survey** and the **US Forest Service** for making some great maps, **Gary Johnson** for getting me out on the Big River, **Taiowa & Michaela** for being my sweet children, **Stacey Flowerdew** for sustenance and cajoling me back to the computer to finish, **Jim Woodward** of **California Parks & Recreation** for his aerial photography, **Steve** and **Lito** at **Northstar Printing** for doing such a great job on the cover, and a special tip of the paddle to **Bruce Herring** for proofreading, editing and being a good friend.

Contents

Introduction

Paddler's Paradise

I was born and raised in San Francisco less than a mile from the beach. I could see the ocean from my bedroom window for 18 years. In this book we are going to travel the California coastline in search of paddleable waters. The waterways we will discover are truly a paddler's paradise.

The Coastal Enviroment

The California coastline is a magical, majestic environment. The ever-present sound of pounding surf, the rugged sea-sculpted rocks seen through the mystical fog, the invigorating smell of the salty sea air; all contribute to the sensual atmosphere that make being at the Pacific Ocean a refreshing and awakening experience. Nearly all destinations listed in this book have beach access for walking, tide pool exploration and, depending on the time of the year, watching the sun set in brilliant shades of red, yellow, orange, blue and violet (or the fog turning darker shades of gray).

All of these bodies of water would be considered "quiet" water. They are appropriate for all levels of paddling skill and are suitable for recreational kayaks, sea kayaks, canoes and inflatables. My criteria for which waterways I included in this book was simple. First, the waterway had to have two wheel drive access via public lands. I excluded waterways that required four wheel drive or whose access required trespassing on private land. Destinations where the put-in is public but the main body of water is surrounded by private lands are noted. Respect people's privacy and we will be able to continue our adventures in these waters. Second, I ended up with is this diverse collection of river mouths, deltas, lagoons, reservoirs, bays, marshes, creeks, and sloughs from the Smith River up near the Oregon border to Morro Bay on the Central coast. South of Morro Bay to the Mexican border there wasn't much in the way of paddleable coastal waterways.

Whether your pleasure is investigating the shore of a fog shrouded lagoon, navigating the twists and turns of a tidal estuary or getting your strokes in on the

"Ah, the ocean, the graceful contours of the coast, where the waves seductively beckon the earth to join the sea, to dance to the timeless rhythms of the tides, creating the beauty of the shoreline."

The Author

1

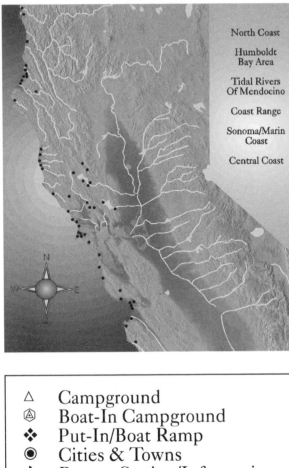

North Coast

Humboldt
Bay Area

Tidal Rivers
Of Mendocino

Coast Range

Sonoma/Marin
Coast

Central Coast

△ Campground
⬡ Boat-In Campground
❖ Put-In/Boat Ramp
◉ Cities & Towns
⬆ Ranger Station/Information
⬛ Lodge
⬭ Interstate Highway
⬭ State Highway
⬭ County Road
▬▬▬ River/Creek
─────── Paved Road
- - - - - - Gravel/Dirt Road
·········· Trail
▭ Open Water

open water of a bay, you will find your paddler's paradise within the pages of this book.

Using This   Using this book is easy. Read it, find a body of water on which you wish to

Book   paddle, and go there. Although the listings in this book will give you a thorough image of what you can expect of a place, there is nothing like being there and doing you own explorations.

Maps   There is a map for each listing which will give you an idea of the shape and proportions of any given location and the surrounding vicinity. The map legend at left has the symbols you need to find your way around on the maps. Every attempt has been made to make the maps as accurate as possible using the most up-to-date resources available. The maps are not meant to be exact. They will give a good idea of where things are located. However, there may be some small discrepancies, and an updated brochure or map from a local information source is your best bet for exact locations. See the *Resources* section of each listing.

Pictures   I have included in every listing photographs of the location in order to give you a visual reference. However, the true beauty of a place can never be known until you see it for yourself.

Description   This section gives you a basic idea of the setting-size of the water body, and any special features you might like to check out.

Camping   This section tells you where in the area you can pitch your tent and cook your meals. It tells you what conveniences and amenities are available, whether or not you need to make a reservation or pay a fee, and whether or not the campground is open year round. Campgrounds run the gambit between a semi-flat place to pitch a tent with a fire-ring to full amenities with flush toilets and hot showers. Some campgrounds can be reserved through Destinet. Destinet has a service charge on top of the campground fee. They can be reached at: 800-283-CAMP.

Many areas have vacation cabin rentals that are available by the day or the week. These can be a nice alternative to camping out, especially during inclement weather. A list of available rentals can usually be obtained from the local Chamber of Commerce.

Directions   It's hard to get someplace if you don't have directions. This section will tell you how to get there and the most convenient place to park your car and where to put your boat in the water. Sometimes it's a boat ramp, sometimes it's a beach, sometimes it's a precarious walk down moss covered rocks or through knee-deep mud.

Resources   This section will tell you what maps, brochures or guide books are available for the area listed. They include U.S.Geological Survey "topo" maps that show the details of the topography, U.S.Forest Service maps that cover large areas, specialty maps produced by private map makers, books and brochures that cover specific areas, and some river guide maps that detail the difficulty of the rapids, where to put in, and where to take out.

The best all around map resources are De Lorme's *Northern California Atlas & Gazette* and *Southern California Atlas & Gazette*. These books contain topo maps for all of California and cover all of the locations listed in *Paddling Northern California*. The most updated maps tend to be the U.S.Forest Service maps of national forests. They don't cover all of the places listed in the book, but they are very accurate and fairly inexpensive. You should also get a good map or atlas of California roadways. The American Automobile Association and Rand McNally both make good road maps.Since most of the listings in this book are on the coast, and thereby affected by the tides, it is crucial that you have a tide schedule of low and high tides.

Most of these resources can be obtained at your local outdoor recreation or book store. See *Appendix A: Suggested Reading; Maps & Guide Books*, page xx, for resource ordering information.

Advisory   This section serves to warn you of any dangers or problems you might encounter including regular windy conditions, power boat traffic, strong tidal and river currents, availability of drinking water, and anything else that might prove to be a problem if you are unprepared.

Information   This section will give you someone to contact about the availability of campsites,

"And so... quietly as the coming dawn, we entered the solitude of the ocean. And if we were not annihilated by the contemplation of such a vast adventure it was by grace of that wise providence of man's nature which, to preserve his reason, lets him be thoughtless before immensity."

Rockwell Kent (1882-1971 American Writer & Artist

"The sea is feline. It licks your feet its huge flanks purr very pleasant for you, but will crack your bones and eat you, for all that, and wipe the crimsoned foam from its jaws as if nothing had happened."

Oliver Wendell Holmes

water levels, current weather & road conditions, etc. They will often have a brochure or map available.

Paddling Safety

Proper Training

When paddling there are two basic skills that you must know, how to paddle and how to swim. In many areas groups like the Red Cross offer instruction in swimming and certified paddling classes. Classes are available for beginning paddling, intermediate river paddling and advanced whitewater paddling. Call your local Red Cross for classes in your area. Many paddle sport stores also offer instruction on paddling and kayaking skills It also pays to thoroughly read a good basic paddling book that covers types of boats, paddle strokes, paddling equipment and other useful information specific to paddle sports.

Personal Flotation Devices

A personal flotation device (PFD) is what we all used to call a life preserver. It keeps you afloat when you're in the water. The only kind worth wearing is a vest style, Coast Guard approved, Type III PFD. The "horse collar" style life preservers should be avoided. They tend to scratch your neck and don't really supply adequate flotation. The law says you should wear a PFD at all times when you're on the water. You should always have a PFD available. Young children, whitewater paddlers, and poor swimmers should always wear PFD whenever they are on or near the water, no exceptions.

Power Boat Wakes

One of the most potentially dangerous hazards of paddling is power boats. You will find them on almost every lake, bay or river mouth that allows them, particularly in the summer months. They are usually, but not always, driven by polite, considerate, sober people. They might not see you and can run you down or tip you over with their wakes. The best way to handle power boats is to stay out of their way. When there are lots of power boats about, stay near the shoreline. Power boats tend to stay in deeper water when they are running at high speeds. When a big wake bears down on you, try to avoid taking it broadside. If you turn into the wake at about a 45 degree angle, it will lessen the side to side rocking effect. If you are paddling into or out of a camp-

Natural Disasters

site on a lake or reservoir, leave early in the morning, when the water is calm, before the wind comes up and the power boats get out on the water. One of the main reasons we paddle is so we can get out into nature. The beauty and grandeur inspire a sense of awe and wonder. There are those times, however, when we must realize that we are not only a part of nature, but a very "small" part. Weather, wind and storm runoff in particular, can radically change the "safety" of any paddle trip. Consider the conditions of the moment and use common sense when deciding to paddle or not to paddle. The natural world is way bigger than we are. Nature will most often heal us, but it can hurt us and even kill us.

Strong river current and the flow of the tides can take away control of your boat and dump you right in the water. Once you are in the water you are subject to the dangers of hypothermia and drowning. Drowning is where you breathe water instead of air, a practice best left to fish. Hypothermia is where your body temperature drops way below normal. You can slip into a coma and die if you don't deal with it correctly and immediately. You can get hypothermia when you get wet. Water as warm as 55 degrees can suck the heat out of your body in a very short time. In very cold water you can lose control of your limbs in as little as five minutes. The ocean water off the coast of northern California is always 55 degrees or colder. Some of the inland waters get a little warmer, but not by much. If you get dunked in cold water, get out and get warm and dry as quickly as possible. For proper treatment of hypothermia see a first aid book or, better yet, take a first aid training class. With proper training and equipment, a warm fire, and a dry set of clothes, these dangers can be easily avoided.

Swift Currents

Rivers on their way to the sea and the tides flowing in and out of bays and lagoons can create a huge volume of moving water. The currents near the mouth of a large river or the inlet of a bay or lagoon can be swift and dangerous. It can be very much like paddling on a class III whitewater river which can carry you out into the ocean. The ocean is definitely not considered quiet water. Check river mouths out visually before you attemp to paddle them. If you are not experienced with whitewater paddling avoid inlets and river mouths altogether.

"A river flowing into the ocean is a powerful image and a potentially dangerous reality"

The Author

"The wind shows us how close to the edge we are."

Joan Didion

"I have a seashell collection: maybe you've seem it. I keep it scattered on beaches all over the world."

Steven Wright, Commedian

Blustery Coastal Winds

Another primordial force to be reckoned with at the ocean is wind. Most days at the ocean there will be some wind, particularly in the afternoons. The onshore winds coming off the ocean can be total misery if you have to paddle into them. Wind can also raise considerable waves on waters that are openly exposed. A weather radio will keep you updated on the current wind and weather conditions with forecasts of winds to come.

Tidal Mud Flats

Tidal mud flats are beautiful and rich environments, teaming with life. They can also be very dangerous if try to walk on them. You can sink in up to your waist, get stuck and when the tide comes back in the water can rise over your head and...well, you get the picture. Places like Humboldt Bay, Bodega Bay, Drakes Estero, Bolinas Lagoon and Morro Bay have large mud flats which are exposed at low tide. The tide can go out so fast that you can be left high and dry before you know it. I talked to a guy who got stranded 50 feet from the water channel on south San Francisco Bay. His choices; wait 12 hours for the tide to come back in, get out and walk/get stuck in the mud or tie the boat to his foot, roll out of the kayak and slither through the stinky mud to the channel. To this day his car still smells of bay mud. Whenever you paddle on coastal waters that are affected by the tides, it is important to carry a tide chart with you. This indispensible resource will tell you when the high tides and low tides are due and just how high or low they will be.

The Coastal Environment

The Changing Seasons

The weather on the coast tends to change almost daily as opposed to season ally. Yes, the winter tends to be colder and wetter. But you can have a warm clear day in February, just as easily as you can freeze your butt off in the fog in August. So in the winter don't forget to bring shorts and in the summer don't forget your coat. Rain, wind, fog, heat and cold, all have their place and season. Whenever you visit the coast you have to be prepared for every possible weather condition.

In springtime the weather can be very unpredictable, running the gambit between cold, windy rain to sunny and quite warm. Rivers are ususally reaching their capacity. Full lakes are great, full rivers can be very dangerous. A river that is a class I or II in the late summer can be unrunnable during spring run-off. Always try to get current information on rivers before you go paddling on them. Some spring days on the coast are cold and windy with the rain coming at you like a fire hose. And then, there are those spring days when the wildflowers reach for the sun as it rises towards its apex, and the water lies glassy on a windless day-you'll swear you're in heaven and you'll never want to go back to work.

Summer in Northern California brings intolerably hot temperatures inland while the coast tends to be shrouded in cool marine fog. Summer also brings the hoards of vacationers. During the summer, if you want to paddle in solitude, you'll have to work for it, and drive the extra miles on the bumpier roads (or be really lucky).

Early Fall on the Northern California coast brings the delight of "indian summer," when the temperatures get into the '70s and the high clouds put on an art show of unparalled beauty, and oohh the sunsets, "Red sky at night, paddler's delight." One of the best paddling adventures of the fall months lies in the wetlands of the coast where water foul come spend their winters. Late fall usually starts the wet rainy season. In the words of Forest Gump, "You never know what you're gonna get."

Winter on the coast brings wind and rain. It can also be the best time of year to get away from the crowds. If you can head out on an adventure at a moment's notice when the rain and wind abate, you can often find a place all to yourself.

No matter what the season, if you get the urge to paddle, you can find the perfect place as you go "Paddling The California Coast".

"The coldest winter I ever spent was the Summer in San Francisco."

Mark Twain

"The Great Sea has set me adrift. It moves me as the weed in a Great River. Earth and the Great Weather move me; have carried me away, and move my inward parts with joy."

Uvavnuk, an Eskimo Woman

What To Bring

Paddle Boat   Paddle boats come in a variety of shapes, sizes and construction materials. What kind of boat you get depends on what kind of paddling you want to do. A boat that holds a good straight line on a lake might not turn very well on a moving, windy river. A boat that is great for casual day trips when all you have to carry are two people and a knapsack might not be big enough for paddle-in camping when you have to carry all your camping gear and food for a couple of days. A good book on basic paddling will cover all the variables (see *Appendix A*, page 80, for a listing of paddling books). Canoe and kayak stores often have demonstration days where you can try out a variety of canoes, recreational kayaks, inflatables, surf kayaks, whitewater kayaks and sea kayaks.

Paddles   The main criteria for a paddle is that it be the right size for you. Standing up with the tip of the paddle on the ground in front of you, the end of the handle should come to about your chin. This will allow you to paddle comfortably with the paddle at the right depth for efficient propulsion through the water. If you're a beginner, paddle design won't matter all that much at first; be it beaver tail, laminated, carbon fiber, one piece, two piece or whatever. You can save all that rigmarole for when you become a total paddling fanatic (it takes about one month). Also, paddle boat demo days usually have a variety of paddles to try.

Clothing   Clothing is very important in paddling. You want to be able to warm up or cool off. Several available layers are the way to go. If you think you might get wet, you should get into synthetics such as poly-propylene underwear, pile sweaters and nylon windbreakers and pants. Wet cotton will drain your body heat away in a hurry, and will leave you vulnerable to hypothermia. Wool becomes heavy and cumbersome when it gets wet (it smells bad, too). Synthetics are lightweight, comfortable, warm when layered, and dry quickly when they get wet. Check at your local paddle sport store. Also, online and mail order camping supply companies have excellent prices on synthetic camp clothing.

Car Racks

Although paddling the backwaters of your garage or yard can be a hoot, it's more fun if you actually take your boat and put it on water. Hence the necessity for boat-carrying racks on your car or truck. You can get a foam block and strap kit for under $25.00 or you can spend hundreds of dollars for the multi-faceted, super-yuppie, deluxe car racks that not only will carry your canoe, snow skis and bicycles, but it will also cook your food and guarantee nice weather.

If you're going to adventure out away from your boat and you want it to be there when you get back, make sure you can lock it down. No, this is not being paranoid, paddle boats really do get stolen. A lock and chain through the rack and the thwart will do, as long as you have the kind of car rack that locks to your car.

Boat

Forgetable Necessities

I hate to sound like your mother, but don't forget your sunscreen. There are a few miscellaneous necessities that everyone needs and almost everyone forgets at one time or another-something to eat, drinking water or a good water filter, sun screen, sunglasses, a hat, clothes to keep you warm and a change of clothes in case you get wet. All of these items should be in waterproof dry bags, specially made for this purpose, in case you capsize.

"...the sea, once it casts its spell, holds one in its net of wonder forever."

Jaques Yves Cousteau

Whatever your paddling pleasure, I hope
this book helps guide you to an
enjoyable time on the water.

The North Coast

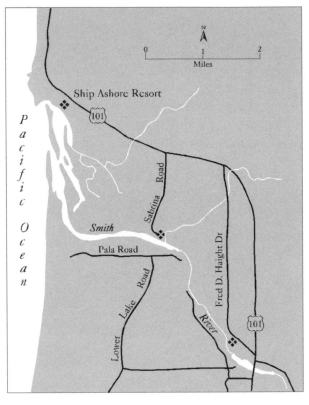

Smith River Mouth   *Courtesy CDPR*

Mouth Of The Smith River

Description   The Smith River is part of California's Wild & Scenic River System and has the distinction of being the last free flowing river in California (no dams). The mouth of the Smith River is a delta area of exquisite beauty and consists of six different habitats, including open water, tidal flats, sand dunes, riparian woodland, river channels and salt marsh.. You can paddle through the delta area at the mouth of the river about 2 miles up from where the river meets the ocean.

The wildlife is abundant

Camping   Ship Ashore RV Park is right at the mouth of the Smith River with a separate tent area, flush toilets, showers, tables, fire grills, laundromat, gas station and restuarant; reservations accepted, call for fees at 707-487-3141. See also, Lake Earl Wildlife Area, *(next page).*

Directions   Take Hwy 101 about 8.5 miles north of Crescent City to the Mouth of the Smith River. Public boat access is available at the end of Sabrina Road off Hwy 101. At this put-in the current is swift; you can drift down stream but it's hard to paddle back up stream; arrange to shuttle back to your car. Ship Ashore Park has a private boat ramp if your staying at the park; ask permission to use the ramp if you're not a guest.

Resources   Six Rivers Nationl Forest map from the USFS; Redwood National Park/North Coast State Parks/Smith River National Recreation Area map from Trails Illustrated; Smith River topo map from USGS; Smith River Fishing Map from Stream Time.

Advisory   There can be significant turbulence where the river meets the ocean. The area is greatly affected by tidal flows. Strong spring currents and afternoon onshore winds. Watch for water skiing power boats in the delta area.

Information   Smith River National Recreation Area; Gasquet Ranger Station, 707-457-3131

Lake Earl Wildlife Area

Description The Lake Earl Wildlife area covers 5,000 acres including Lake Earl and smaller Lake Talawa. Both are shallow fresh water lagoons covering an area of about 2,000 acres. The two lagoons are surrounded by salt and freshwater marshes, and groves of Sitka spruce and red alder which serve as home for an abundance of waterfowl and other animals. Over 250 species of birds live and migrate through this oceanside wetlands including; canvas back and Aleutian Canada geese, trundra swans, black bellied plovers, peregrine falcons, bald eagles, and more than eighty different songbirds.The marshes and creeks support a wide variety of mammals including muskrats, beavers and river otters. Grey whales, sea lions and harbor seals can often be seen from the beach.

Camping Lake Earl campground is a walk-in camp about a half mile north of Lake Earl with tables, fire rings, composting toilets and food lockers, (bring your own water); for a fee, register at Jedediah Smith or Del Norte State Parks. Other campgrounds include; Jedediah Smith State Park, Del Norte Coast State Park, Gold Bluffs Beach State Park, Prarie Creek. *(See also, camping for Smith River, previous page.)*

Directions Take Hwy 101 north from Crescent City to Northcrest Drive; veer left and go about 2 miles; turn left on Old Mill Road; follow signs to the Lake Earl Wildlife Area. Public boat accesses are located at Teal Point in the Pacific Shores subdivision south off Kellogg Rd, at the end of Lake View Drive and at the end of Buzzini Road.

Resources: Six Rivers National Forest map from USFS; Redwood National Park/North Coast State Parks/Smith River National Recreation Area map from Trails Illustrated; Crescent City USGS topo map.

Advisory The current between the two lakes can get pretty swift during higher tides. The middle of Lake Earl can get very windy without much warning. If you don't like guns avoid duck hunting season. The heavy north coast winter rains can make for an extremely dismal experience.

Information Department Of Fish & Game 707-464-2523

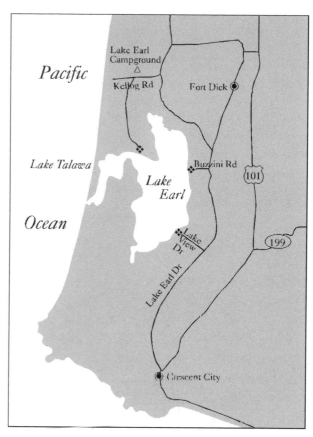

Lake Earl & Lake Talawa   *Courtesy CDPR*

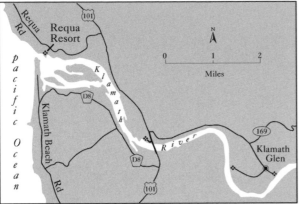

The Mighty Klamath River meets the sea

Klamath River Mouth from the air   Courtesy CDPR

Mouth Of The Klamath River

Description   The Klamath is a long river flowing hundreds of miles from southern Oregon. It has an extremely high flow volume year round. Even at the mouth the current is quite strong. Paddling upstream is exhausting. Your best bet is to put-in upstream a few miles, ride the current down and then shuttle back to your car.

Camping   The best camping in the area is in one of the campgrounds at Prairie Creek Redwoods State Park to the south; either Elk Prairie or Gold Bluff Beach. Elk Prairie has 75 campsites with water, flush toilets, tables, fire rings, and showers. The most remarkable feature of this site is the presence of Roosevelt elk herds. It is rare that one can get so close to such a magnificent animal. Why hang out with recreational vehicles when you can hang out with Roosevelt elk. Reserve thru Destinet 800-444-7275 for a fee. Gold Bluff Beach is a beautiful campground with 27 campsites, water, flush toilets, fire rings, tables, and solar showers (if the sun ain't shinin' you'll just have to bathe in cold water) Some of the hikes through fern covered creekbeds near the campgrounds are spectacular. No reservations; fee required; call Prairie Creek Redwood State Park at 707-488-2171

Directions   Follow the signs on Hwy 101 south of Crescent City. You can't miss the Klamath River. The best put-in for a float down to the mouth of the river is to take Hwy 169 east off Hwy 101 to Klamath Glenn, go to the Roy Rook Public Boat Ramp where there is a paved ramp into a calm eddy in the river. It's a safe, easy put-in. Be sure to arrange a shuttle back to your car.

Resources   Six Rivers National Forest map from USFS; Redwood National Park/North Coast State Parks/Smith River National Recreation Area map from Trails Illustrated; Requa topo map from the USGS; *Handbook Of The Klamath* by Quinn.

Advisory   Very strong currents can carry you downstream before you know it. Paddlers should have some experience with swift moving water.

Information   None.

Upstream on the Klamath River

Stone Lagoon

Freshwater Lagoon

Humboldt Lagoons State Park~Freshwater, Stone & Big Lagoons   *Courtesy CDPR*

Stone Lagoon   *Courtesy CDPR*

Big Lagoon

Humboldt Lagoons State Park

Description Humboldt Lagoons State Park is a series of three lagoons; Freshwater Lagoon, Stone Lagoon and Big Lagoon; nestled among the forests and beaches of the northern California coast. Big Lagoon offers paddling through salt water marshes and Stone Lagoon offers paddle-in camping. Try paddling or walking along the spit at sunset, (or in the fog). Aprroximately 17 miles south of Stone Lagoon is the Little River, a short little paddle in the redwoods.

Camping Stone Lagoon paddle-in campground is on the inland side of the hill that separates the lagoon from the ocean. There are six 6 tent sites with pit toilets, fire rings, and tables for a fee. There is no water so bring your own. No pets allowed. No reservations are required.

Stone Lagoon campground lies at the north end of the lagoon has 25 environmental campsites with tables, pit toilets, fire rings, food locker, but no water for a fee. No reservations

Dry Lagoon campground at the south end of Big Lagoon has 6 primitive campsites with tables, pit toilets, fire rings, but no water for a fee. No reservations

Directions South of Crescent City on Highway 101 to the Redwood Information Center, just south of Orick. From there drive 3 miles south to the parking lots. From the boat ramp it's about 3/4 of a mile to the boat-in camp .

Resources Six Rivers National Forest map from USFS; Redwood National Park/North Coast State Parks/Smith River National Recreation Area map from Trails Illustrated; Orrick, Rodgers Peak & Trinidad USGS topo maps.

Advisory Get on the water early. High on shore winds can make for choppy water in the after-noons.

Information Prarie Creek Redwoods State Park, 707-488-2171

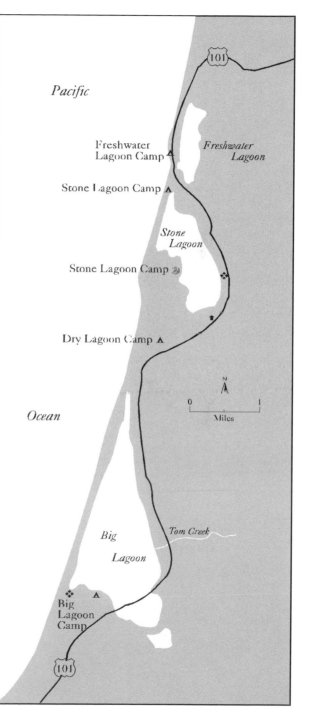

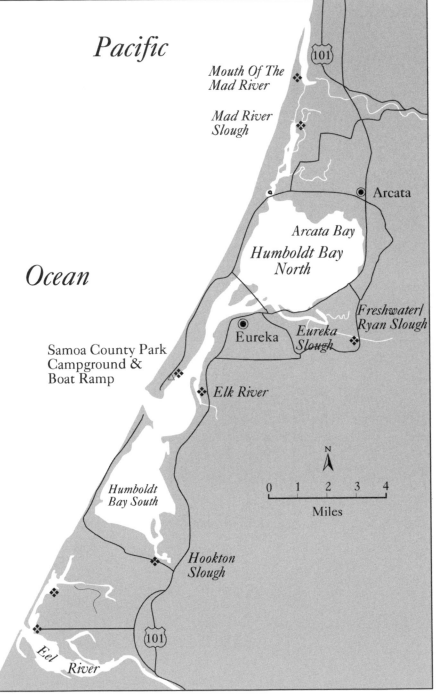

Humboldt Bay Area

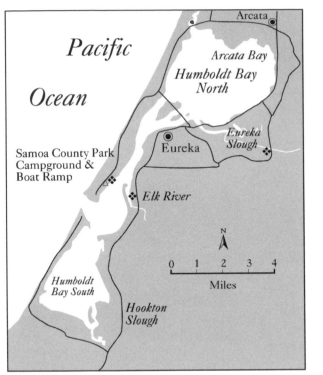

Humboldt Bay from the air   Courtesy CDPR

Humboldt Bay

Description   Humboldt Bay is the second largest bay in California. Wildlife abounds all around the bay including harbor seals, heron, brown pelican, tundra swans, black brants, American bittern, clams and crabs just to name a very few. If you like big water this is the place for you. Humboldt Bay encompasses almost 13,000 acres of water. It would take days to explore its shoreline. You would experience highly industrialized logging, commercial and recreational fishing, pristine marshes and mud flats and more wildlife encounters than you can shake a stick at.

Camping   Clam Beach County Park is the nicest campground in the area for location. Right on the beach, this campground has 50 campsites with vault toilets and water for a fee; no reservations. Samoa Boat Launch County Park has ten campsites for tents and lots of RV spaces with flush toilets, water, tables, fire grills, a grocery store, and a laundromat for a fee; no reservations; for information call 707-445-7652. Sometimes your best bet in this area is an inexpensive motel room.

Directions   Humboldt Bay sits right next to Highway 101. There are several access points around the bay: one boat ramp in the town of Fields Landing, three boat ramps in the city of Eureka and two boat ramps off of the Samoa Peninsula near the north jetty.

Resources   For all of Humboldt Bay; Tyee City, Arcata North, Eureka, Arcata South, Cannibal Island, and Fields Landing topo maps from the USGS. *Humboldt Bay Area Bike Map* published by Natural Resources Services Division of Redwood Community Action Agency, 707-269-2060, covers Arcata Bay in great detail.

Advisory   The middle of Humboldt Bay is not a particularly safe place to paddle. There is lots of boat traffic, including BIG ships. If ocean winds come up strong, you can be a long way from the safety of the shore in 2-3 foot waves with little control of your boat. Keep an eye on the tides. Many areas of Humboldt and Arcata Bays are greatly affected by the tides. It is easy to get stranded on the many mud flats in the area, especially in Arcata Bay. Don't walk in the mud you WILL get stuck. It is also crucial to avoid the inlet to the bay. The tidal flow is very swift and the ocean swells come in straight off the ocean and often break in the channel as they hit shallower water. The Humboldt Bay channel is definitely NOT quiet water. Stay away from the Humboldt Bay Nuclear Power Plant. Even though it is decommisioned, it is still off limits.

Information   Humboldt Bay National Wildlife Area, 707-733-5406; Nature Conservancy, 707-822-6378.

Mad River

Description   The Mad River estuary is a perfect quiet water paddle. If you get on the Mad River when the tide is rising you can go either upstream or downstream. The paddle upstream 'til you meet the current then downstream to the mouth of the river and back to the boat ramp is about an 8-10 mile paddle round trip; definitely a full day of exploration. Further upstream is a seasonal Class I whitewater run. At the mouth of the river you can take a long walk along either Mad River Beach to the south or Clam Beach to the north. There is ample opportunity to view wildlife and flora including river otter, snowy plover, American prairie falcon, bush lupine, Sitka spruce and black cottonwood.

Camping   Clam Beach County Park is right on the beach and has 50 campsites with vault toilets, and water for a fee; no reservations There are many inexpensive motels in the area.

Directions   To get to the Mad River, take Highway 101 north of Arcata to Janes Road exit. Turn right on Heindon Road to left on Miller Lane to right on Mad River Road; park and put-in at the boat ramp. The mouth of the river is accessible by walking south from Clam Beach County Park.

Resources   Tyee City and Arcata North topo maps from the USGS; *Humboldt Bay Area Bike Map* published by Natural Resources Services Division of Redwood Community Action Agency, 707-269-2060.

Advisory   Onshore winds can make paddling difficult especially in a canoe. Where the river meets the ocean can be very dangerous.

Information   Mad River Beach County Park 707-445-7652, Nature Conservancy, 707-822-6378.

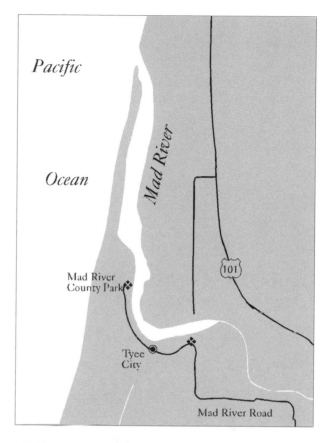

The Mad River estuary is perfect paddlers of all kinds

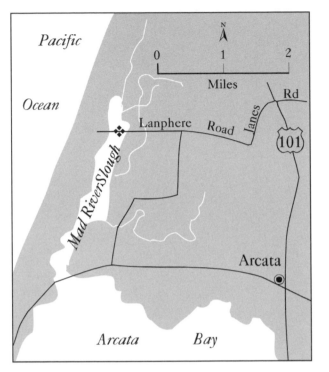

Mad River Slough

Description Mad River Slough is at the northwest end of Humboldt Bay and offers a great paddling adventure in a tidal estuary/salt marsh/sand dune environment. This area contained within the Mad River Slough and Dunes Management Area consists of seven distinct ecosystems. There is an exceptional diversity of bird populations. The Humboldt Bay National Wildlife Refuge offers weekend guided tours of Lanphere/Christensen Dunes Preserve right next to Mad River Slough.

Camping See "Humboldt Bay", page 20.

Directions To get on the Mad River Slough, take Highway 101 north of Eureka, take the Guintoli Road exit, go west on Guintoli Road to left on Upper Bay Road, stay straight as Upper Bay Road turns into Lanphere Road, you will come to the Mad River Slough at the bridge.

Resources Eureka, Tyee City, Arcata North topo maps from the USGS; *Humboldt Bay Area Bike Map* published by Natural Resources Services Division of Redwood Community Action Agency, 707-269-2060.

Advisory Keep an eye on the tides. You must get on and off the water at or near high tide to avoid a mud walk which could get you dangerously stuck in the mud. This area is greatly affected by the tides. It is easy to get stranded upstream in a slough or grounded on the many mud flats in the area. Paddling out into Humboldt Bay can be dangerous, especially for canoes.

Information Humboldt Bay National Wildlife Area, 707-733-5406; Nature Conservancy, 707-822-6378.

Beautiful flora abound on the Mad River Slough

Eureka, Fay, Ryan & Freshwater Sloughs

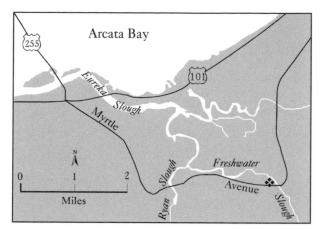

Description   Eureka Slough and its tributaries create an intricate and varied system of water-ways that wander through city canals, marshes and pasturelands. Being a saltwater/freshwater marsh environment, the area is populated by anadromous fish, amphibians, waterfowl, song birds and small mammals.

Camping   See "Humboldt Bay", page 20.

Directions   The easiest put-in I found for this area was onto Freshwater Slough off Myrtle Avenue. From Highway 101 in Eureka go southeast on Myrtle Avenue until it crosses Freshwater Slough just past the developed part of town.

Resources   Fields Landing topo map from the USGS; *Humboldt Bay Area Bike Map* published by Natural Resources Services Division of Redwood Community Action Agency, 707-269-2060.

Advisory   Keep an eye on the tides. You must get on and off the water at or near high tide to avoid a mud walk which could get you dangerously stuck in the mud. This area is greatly affected by the tides. It is easy to get stranded upstream in a slough or grounded on the many mud flats in the area. Paddling out into Humboldt Bay can be dangerous, especially for canoes.

Information   Humboldt Bay National Wildlife Area, USFWS, 707-733-5406.

Isolated, pristine and intimate Ryan Slough

Long and wide Freshwater Slough

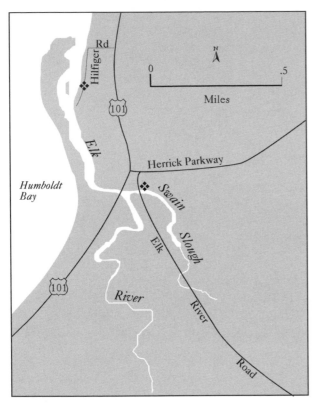

Elk River

Description The Elk River is Humboldt Bay's largest tributary. It used to be surrounded by large redwood forests, but was logged out in the 1800's. It is now surrounded by houses and pastures and farmland, although, the river often overflows its levees in winter providing seasonal marshes for wildlife.. The riverbank is leveed for three and a half miles upstream from the bay. Over the years a sand spit has formed, extending about a mile into Humboldt Bay. The spit supports sparse vegetation inhabited by songbirds, reptiles and rodents. Predatory birds like ospreys, northern harriers and black-shouldered kites can be seen hovering skyward searching for a meal.

Camping See "Humboldt Bay", page 20.

Directions From Highway 101 just south of Eureka turn west on Hilfiker Lane to the parking lot at the trailhead for the Elk River City Wildlife Area. That's the put-in.

Resources Eureka and Fields Landing topo maps from the USGS; *Humboldt Bay Area Bike Map* published by Natural Resources Services Division of Redwood Community Action Agency, 707-269-2060.

Advisory Keep an eye on the tides. You must get on and off the water at or near high tide to avoid a mud walk which could get you dangerously stuck in the mud. This area is greatly affected by the tides. It is easy to get stranded upstream in a slough or grounded on the many mud flats in the area. Paddling out into Humboldt Bay can be dangerous, especially for canoes.

Information Humboldt Bay National Wildlife Area, USFWS, 707-733-5406.

Low tide on the Elk River⁰

Hookton Slough

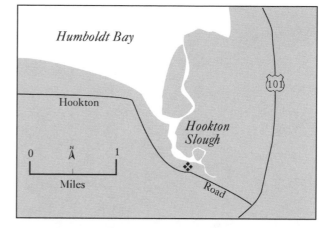

Description   Hookton Slough is part of the Humboldt Bay National Wildlife Refuge. The South Bay area is for the most part undeveloped. A dike at the bay end of Hookton Slough was removed to allow the former marshland to recover. The slough is home to great variety of wildlife including: herons, ducks, osprey, egrets, harbor seals, Dungeness crabs and many more species too numerous to mention.

Camping   See "Humboldt Bay", page 20.

Directions   From Highway 101 south of Eureka take the Hookton Road exit, go west on Hookton Road to the parking lot on the north side of the road next to the slough.

Resources   Fields Landing topo map from USGS; map from Humboldt Bay National Wildlife Refuge, 707-733-5406.

Advisory   Keep an eye on the tides. You must get on and off the water at or near high tide to avoid a mud walk which could get you dangerously stuck in the mud. This area is greatly affected by the tides. It is easy to get stranded upstream in a slough or grounded on the many mud flats in the area. Paddling out into Humboldt Bay can be dangerous, especially for canoes.

Information   Humboldt Bay National Wildlife Refuge, 707-733-5406.

Egret feeding in Hookton Slough

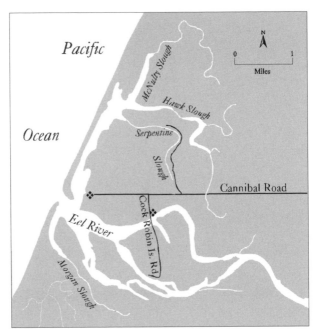

Mouth Of The Eel River

Description   This is a large area of sloughs, marshes, mud flats, and tidal channels. Cock Robin Island is home to sea lions and occasionally seals or river otters. You'll also find a wide variety of seabirds, songbirds and waterfowl. Like all delta/estuaries, the Eel River delta is a prime area for discovery. The Eel River runs slower than the Klamath and paddling upstream is not too strenuous. At high tides there are many tributaries, big and small to explore.

Camping   See "Humboldt Bay", page 20.

Directions   From Highway 101 south of Eureka take the Loleta exit; go west to the Eel River Road; go north to Cannibal Road which dead-ends at a beach with an easy put-in.

Resources   Cannibal Island, Fields Landing, Ferndale and Fortuna topo maps from the USGS; Eel River Fishing Map from Stream Time.

Advisory   There are a lot of places to get stuck here when the tide goes out. Keep an eye on the tide; currents can be tricky where the river meets the ocean. On shore winds can make the trip back down river cold and strenuous.

Information   Eel River Wildlife Area, USFWS, 707-733-5406.

One of the many side sloughs of the Eel River delta

Mouth Of The Mattole River

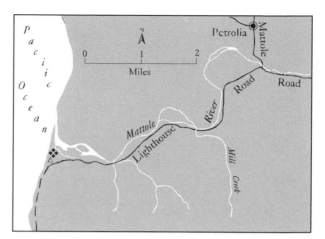

Description This is an out of the way spot. That can often insure solitude, peace and quiet.

Camping The Mouth Of The Mattole campground has 5 campsites and is open year round with tables, fireplaces and vault toilets. Water is available during the summer months only. No reservations. Camping is free.

Directions From Highway 101 south of Eureka take Highway 211 west which turns into Mattole Road; stay on Mattole Road to Petrolia; just south of Petrolia turn west on Lighthouse Road which dead ends at the river mouth. Or, from Highway 101 just north of Weott take the South Fork/Honeydew exit; go west on Mattole Road to just south of Petrolia; turn west on Lighthouse Road which dead ends at the river mouth.

Resources Petrolia and Buckeye Mountain topo maps from USGS

Advisory Bring your own water in fall, winter and spring. Keep an eye on the tide; currents can be tricky where the river meets the ocean. On shore winds can make the trip back down river cold and strenuous. The Mattole River is a long way from a gas station; fill up before you head out.

Information Bureau Of Land Management, 707-822-7648.

Near to nowhere Mattole River mouth　　　*Courtesy of CDPR*

Mattole River mouth from the air　　　*Courtesy of CDPR*

Mattole River Mouth

Weott

101

Pacific

Leggett

1

101

Ten Mile River

McKerricher State Park

Noyo River

Fort Bragg

Russian Gulch State Park

Mendocino

Big River

Van Damme State Park

Albion River

Navaro River

Navarro River Redwoods State Park

Ocean

1

Manchester

Garcia River

Gualala

Gualala River

Tidal Rivers Of Mendocino

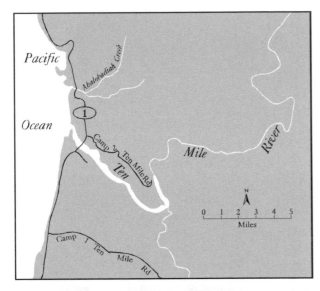

Ten Mile River meets the sea

Ten Mile River's salt water marsh

Ten Mile River

Description Ten Mile River is so named because it lies 10 miles north of Noyo Harbor. Just behind the dunes where the river meets the ocean is a 75 acre salt marsh. Common mergansers and other waterfowl nest in the marsh. Further upstream, about 1 mile inland, Ten Mile River splits into the north and south forks where a wide variety of riparian wildlife can be found. Steelhead trout, silver salmon and Pacific lamprey spawn in the river bottom.

From the mouth of the river you can take a nice 4.5 mile walk south on Ten Mile Beach, one of the longest stretches of dunes in California. Life in these barrier dunes includes endangered plant species Menzies wallflower, Mendocino paintbrush and Thurber's reed grass, along with rare nesting snowy plovers and spawning night smelt.

Also, an easy little paddle can be found on Lake Cleone in MacKerricher State Park.

Camping: MacKerricher State Park is a beautiful oceanside campground. There are 140 campsites with tables, fire-rings, food lockers, flush toilets and showers for a fee. Reservations through Destinet (1-800-283-CAMP). The campground is open year round. Within the park you can go for an easy little paddle on Lake Cleone, or you can go walking on the beach and explore some tide pools (watch out for rogue waves). There are also many vacation rentals in the area for those who wish a softer mattress on which to sleep. Contact the Mendocino County Chamber of Commerce for a brochure of rentals.

Directions From MacKerricher State Park drive north on Hwy 1 about 7 miles to the river; turn into the parking lot on the south end of the bridge on the west side of Hwy 1. There is a trail that leads down to the river side. It is a little difficult to maneuver a canoe overhead through the bushes, but it can be done.

Resources: Inglenook & Dutchman's Knoll topo maps from USGS.

Advisory: The land on both sides of Ten Mile River is privately owned, so respect the owners' privacy. Keep an eye on the tide; currents can be tricky where the river meets the ocean. On-shore winds can make the trip back down river cold and strenuous.

Information: MacKerricher State Park, 707-937-5804.

Noyo River & Harbor

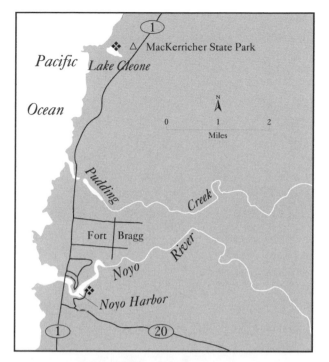

Description   The Noyo River meets the ocean at Noyo Harbor at the south end of Fort Bragg. The Pomo natives used to live here in a village, No-yo-bida, which is how the river got its name. Down river from the put-in this small harbor is teaming with all the activity of the fishing industry: the fishing trollers smelling of diesel motoring in and out; harbor seals, sea gulls and sea lions waiting for scraps of food to be washed off the cannery docks; men in yellow rain suits unloading their catch and maintaining their boats; and, yes, canoers and sea kayakers weaving their way amongst it all.

Upriver lies a placid 5.5 mile paddle into the richly forested environment of a coastal riparian corridor. This tidal estuary is habitat for great blue herons, eagles, seabirds, songbirds, seals and river otters. It is also a wintering area for geese, ducks and migrating shore birds. The river itself is inhabited by Dungeness crabs, striped surfperch, starry flounder and Pacific herring. Steelhead trout, smelt and silver salmon use the river to spawn.

Out of Fort Bragg you can take a rail ride on the Skunk Train which crosses over the Noyo River on its way to Willits. In January, you can take a tour boat out from Noyo Harbor to watch the gray whale migration, or you can watch for the ocean behemoths from Laguna Point in MacKerricher State Park. Also of note in the area is the pygmy forests in Jug Handle and Van Damme State Parks where Bolander and Bishop pines, dwarf cypress, manzanita and huckleberry are stunted in growth due to shallow acidic soil.

Camping   MacKerricher State Park *(see Ten Mile River, Camping, pg 30)*. There are also many vacation rentals in the area for those who wish a softer mattress on which to sleep. Contact the Mendocino County Chamber of Commerce for a brochure of rentals.

Directions   At the south end of the bridge over the Noyo River go east on Hwy 20, then take a left onto South Harbor. There is a public boat ramp at the end of the road.

Resources   Fort Bragg, Noyo Hill and Northspur topo maps from USGS.

Advisory: Keep an eye on the tide; currents can be deceptive where the river meets the ocean. On-shore winds can make the trip back down river cold and strenuous. Don't get too close to the big sea lions. They can get mean and nasty with their territorial attitude, and they are quite a bit bigger than your average canoe.

Information: Jackson State Forest 707-964-5674.

Noyo Harbor

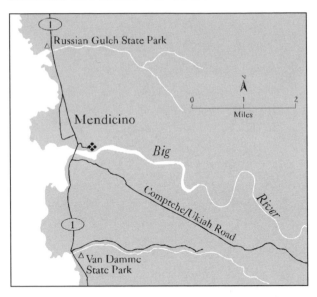

Great blue heron fishing the river bank

Big River

Description The Big River is the paddler's paradise of tidal rivers. If you catch the tide just right you can paddle up river for 8.5 miles. The round trip takes about 6-7 hours. You will definitely get a good night's sleep after this paddle. Along the way you can see river otter, harbor seals, sea lions and great blue heron. Endangered Bald Eagles winter here, and there are some beautiful meadows and marshes up over the banks where you can look for more wildlife and wildflowers.

Be sure to visit the town of Mendocino where you can fuel up for a trip at some great restaurants and coffee shops. The Mendocino Headlands State Park is out at the ocean end of the town with its rugged rocky steep bluffs where winter storm waves erupt in explosive splendor and tide pools team with starfish, mussels, anemones, crabs and other intertidal life forms. Fern trail is a beautiful hike in Van Damme State Park that goes 5 miles up the banks of the Little River.

Camping MacKerricher State Park (*see Ten Mile River, Camping, page 30*). Russian Gulch State Park has 30 campsites with water, flush toilets, fireplaces, tables and showers for a fee. Reserve through Destinet (1-800-283-CAMP), open mid-March through mid-October. Van Damme State Park has 70 campsites with water, flush toilets, tables, showers and fireplaces for a fee. Reserve through Destinet (1-800-283-CAMP). The campground is open all year. There are also many vacation rentals in the area for those who wish a softer mattress on which to sleep. Contact the Mendocino County Chamber of Commerce for a brochure of rentals.

Directions Just on the south side of the town of Mendocino. Turn east down the road on the north side of the bridge over the river, then take the first right into the beach parking area at the foot of the bridge. Don't get stuck in the sand-I saw it happen. Put in right under the bridge. Don't go up the logging road on the north side of the river. Logging trucks come careening down the road, and there is no good river access up stream.

Resources Jackson State Forest map from the CDF; Mendocino, Mathison and Comptche topo maps from USGS.

Advisory Watch for old logging snags submerged in the water. There's an occupied houseboat on the south bank about 3 miles upstream; give the owner his privacy. Keep an eye on the tide; currents can be tricky where the river meets the ocean. On-shore winds can make the trip back down river cold and strenuous.

Information Jackson State Forest 707-964-5674.

Albion River

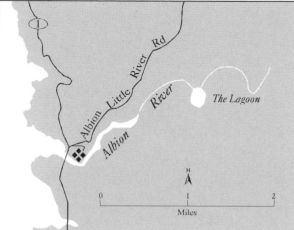

Description A short little float up one the prettiest rivers on the coast. Beds of eel grass sway upriver or downriver pointing in the direction of the tide and lots of redwoods line the shore. Look for golden eagles, osprey, great blue herons, river otter, owls, and sea birds. Harbor seals sun themselves lazily on a little island about a mile inland.

A few miles upstream is an interesting feature known as the lagoon. A small lake-like body of water that fills and empties with the tide. The opening is on the south side of the river and is only about ten feet wide. The tide creates quite a rushing current going in and out of the lagoon.

Camping MacKerricher State Park *(see Ten Mile River, Camping, page 30)*; Van Damme & Russian Gulch State Parks *(see Big River, Camping, previous page 32)*. There are also many vacation rentals in the area for those who wish a softer mattress on which to sleep. Contact the Mendocino County Chamber of Commerce for a brochure of rentals.

Directions About 6 miles south of Mendocino on Hwy 1. Turn east just past the north side of the bridge down to the private harbor. They'll be happy to let you put in there for a small parking fee.

Resources Albion, Elk and Mathison topo maps from USGS.

Advisory Keep an eye on the tide; currents can be misleading where the river meets the ocean. On-shore winds can make the trip back down river cold and strenuous. You have to stay at least fifty feet back from the harbor seals.

Information None Available.

Cord grass waves in the tide

Habor seal sunning on a mid-river island

33

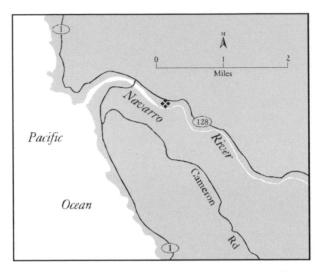

The Navarro River meets the Pacific Ocean

End of the line upriver

Navarro River

Description   The Navarro River is not really a tidal river. The year round flow of the Navarro is enough to keep the tides at bay. From the mouth of the Navarro you can get up river about three and a half miles. During high water flows you can take an exciting trip downriver in swiftly moving class I water from either Hendy Woods State Park, (11 miles to the sea), or Paul W. Dimmick State Park, (9 miles to the sea). If you make the class I run, be sure to arrange a shuttle back to you car from down river.Redwood, bay laurel, tanoak, douglas fir and madrone trees frame the banks of the Navarro.

Hendy Woods also has the distinction of having two virgin redwood groves within its boundries with some trees reaching 300 feet tall and 16 feet in diameter. Be sure to set a spell in the cool shade among these magnificent giants. At the mouth of the Navarro shorebirds hunt for Dungeness crabs which have a nursery there.Upstream you can see stellar jays, great horned owls, pileated woodpeckers, thrushes and common egrets.

Camping   You can camp for free on the beach right at the mouth of the river. These are very primitive campsites with restrooms only, so bring your own water. Take Navarro Bluff Road west off Hwy 1 on the south side of the bridge over the river at the mouth. Paul W. Dimmick Wayside State Campground sits right next to the Navarro River on Hwy 128 about 8 miles in from the coast with 30 campsites with water, tables, toilets and fireplaces for a fee; no reservations.Van Damme State Park, *(see Big River, Camping, page 32)*. There are also many vacation rentals in the area for those who wish a softer mattress on which to sleep. Contact the Mendocino County Chamber of Commerce for a brochure of rentals.

Directions   At the juntion of Hwy 1 and Hwy 128, about 7.5 miles south of the town of Mendocino, go west on Hwy 128. There are a couple of places to park and put-in within one quarter mile of the junction to paddle upriver.

Resources   Albion, Elk, Navarro, Cold Springs and Philo topo maps from USGS; Navarro River Fishing Map from Stream Time.

Advisory   Keep an eye on the tide. During winter and spring rains, river flows can make upstream travel difficult to impossible, and currents are turbulent where the river meets the ocean. On-shore winds can make the trip back down river very chilly.

Information   Hendy Woods, 707-937-5804 or Paul Dimmick State Park, 707-937-5804.

Gualala River

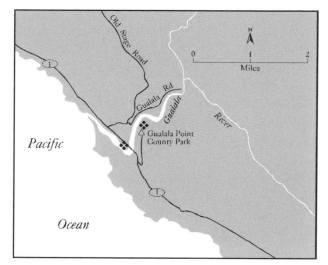

Description   The Gualala River takes an unusual course flowing south to north. You can paddle quite a ways up river in the summer and fall. During spring and winter rains you can travel downriver from Annapolis Rd., 11 miles to the sea on a class I river run. At the coast the Gualala runs by a sandspit, barrier dunes and freshwater marshes. The rushes and cattails of the marsh are home to waterfowl and shorebirds, while the dunes provide a resting places for egrets, herons, and gulls. Further upriver the dunes give way to a conifer forest. Keep an eye out for osprey, skunks, racoons, foxes, river otter and ringtails. Take the time to visit Salt Point State Park about 16 miles to the south. There are numerous tide pools to explore and its rock formations along the coastline range from intricate to magnificent.

Camping   Gualala Point is a beautiful campground set in the redwoods alongside the river. There are 19 developed sites and 6 walk-in environmental sites with tables, fireplaces and restrooms for a fee; no reservations. The Gerstle Cove Campground in Salt Point State Park has 30 developed campsites with tables, fireplaces, water and flush toilets for a fee. Reserve through Destinet (1-800-283-CAMP). The Woodside campground has 79 developed sites, 20 walk-in sites and 10 unimproved sites for a fee. Reserve through Destinet (1-800-283-CAMP). There are also many vacation rentals in the area for those who wish a softer mattress on which to sleep. Contact the Mendocino County Chamber of Commerce for a brochure of rentals.

Directions   Take Hwy 1 about 37 miles north of the Russian River to the town of Gualala. Go west on the dirt road at the south end of the Gualala River Bridge down to the river's edge. From this put-in you can go downstream to the spit or upstream for quite a ways. Or you can put in from Highway 1 in Gualala, then go east on Old Stage Road (Route 505) then right to the river.

Up Stream On The Gualala River

Resources   Gualala, McGuire Ridge and Stewart's Point topo maps from USGS; Gualala River Fishing Map from Stream Time.

Advisory   Keep an eye on the tide. During winter and spring rains, river flows can make upstream travel difficult to impossible and currents are tricky where the river meets the ocean. On-shore winds can make the trip back down river cold and strenuous.

Information   Gualala Point Regional Park, 707-785-2377

The Gualala River Meets The Ocean

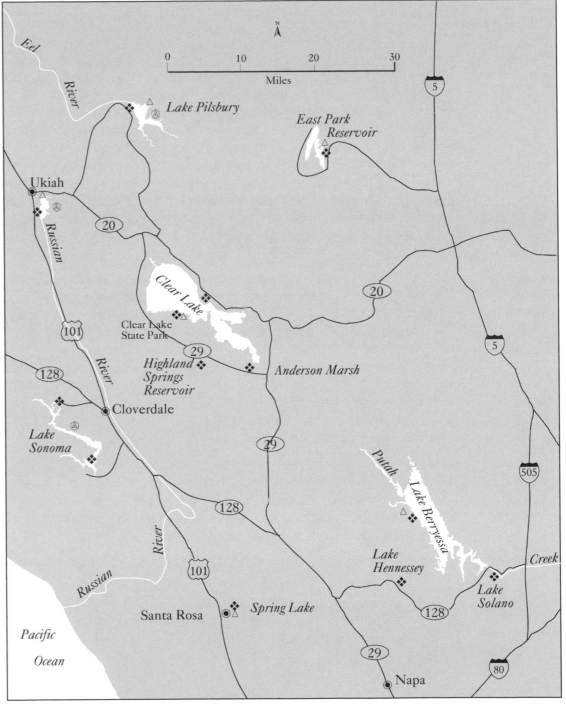

The Coast Range

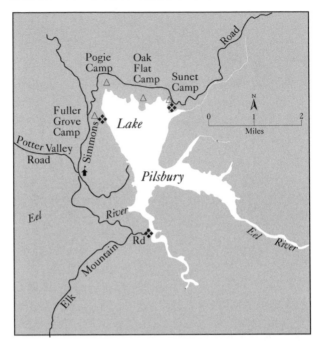

Lake Pilsbury

Description   This beautiful lake is set among pines and oaks at 1,800 feet. Pillsbury Lake is a good sized lake with 65 miles of shoreline and about 2,000 surface acres. There are many coves to explore and the Eel River and Rice Fork arms of the lake offer some close in river like paddling. Hiking trails are also abundant in the surrounding area.

Camping   Fuller Grove has 30 sites with running water, tables, fireplaces and vault toilets for a fee; no reservations. Pogie Point has 50 sites with running water, vault toilets, fireplaces and tables for a fee; no reservations. Oak Flat is a primitive campground with 12 sites, vault toilets, tables, fireplaces and no water. Sunset Campground has 54 sites with running water, vault toilets, tables and fireplaces for a fee; no reservations, (this campground is often used by off road vehicle riders. Lake Pillsbury Resort is a developed campground with 40 sites, running water, flush toilets, showers, tables and fireplaces for a fee; reservations through the resort office 707-743-1581

Directions   From Highway 20 just east of Lake Mendocino go north on East Slide Potter Valley Road north to Eel River Road; go north on Eel River Road; at the Eel River go left, stay on Eel River Road which turns into Elk Mountain Road which goes to the lake and campground. It's easier than it sounds. The dirt part of the road can get pretty muddy and lots of rain in the winter can create wash outs.

Resources   Mendicino National Forest map from USFS; Lake Pillsbury topo map from USGS

Advisory   Watch for power boats.Keep an eye out for rising winds.

Information   USFS Upper Lake Ranger Station, 707-275-2361

Lake Pilsbury has7 several islands to explore

Bald Mountain rises to 6,700 feet to the north of Lake Pilsbury

Lake Mendocino

Description Lake Mendicino sits in the Coyote Valley on the East Fork of the Russian River at 748 ft. It is three miles long and one mile wide. The lake has a boat-in camp on the east side of the lake. At fuller levels you can paddle up the East Fork Russian River at the north end of the lake. The area is populated with red-tailed hawks, grey foxes, valley quail, osprey, wild turkeys and blacktail deer. Nearby are Clear Lake and natural spring fed Blue Lakes.

Camping There are 18 boat-in campsites at the Milti campground with toilets, tables and fireplaces, no fee, no reservations; Che-kaka campground has 22 campsites with toilets, water, tables, fireplaces for a fee, no reservations; Ky-en campground has 103 campsites with flush toilets, water, tables, fireplaces and showers for a fee, no reservations; Bu-shay campgroundhas 164 campsites with flush toilets, water, tables, fireplaces and showers for a fee, no reservations.

Directions Where Hwy 101 meets Hwy 20 near Calpella. There are two public boat ramps located at either Che-kaka or Ky-en campgrounds.

Resources Ukiah topo map from the USGS; www.spn.usace.army.mil/mendocino/

Advisory This is a very popular lake in summer. Watch for power boats. Bring your own water or a water filter to the boat in camp. Hunting is permitted on the east shore from the 3rd Saturday in October throught the last Sunday in February. The catfish in the lake bite! It doesn't hurt, but it'll scare the livin' daylights out of you!

Information Park Manager 707-462-7581

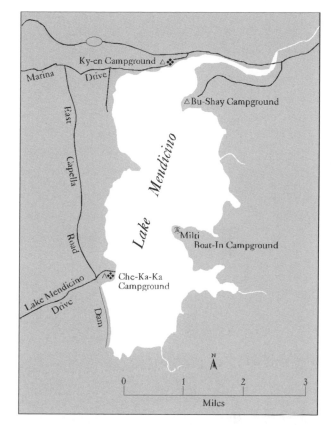

Lake Mendocino is a beautiful color blue

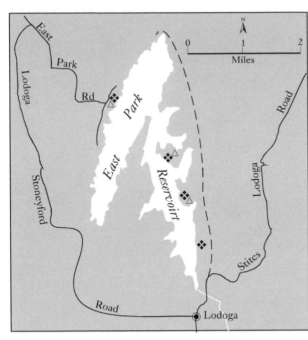

Snow on St. John Mountain north of East Park Reservoir

East Park Reservoir

Description   East Park Reservoir sits at 1,198 feet elevation in the hills on the eastern side of the Coast Range. This is a great winter, spring, early summer lake. During the summer water levels drop quickly turning the lake into a mud puddle, in the middle of a sweltering, dry grassland with no shade. I was there in May, and it was gorgeous: full lake, blue water, green, rolling hills, wild flowers and a dusting of snow on the distant mountains. Power boats of all kinds are allowed on the lakes. However, the shallow coves on the southeastern arm of the lake are great for paddle exploration and are free of power boats.

Camping   There is open camping around most of the lake. There are some picnic tables and some vault toilets scatter around the lake. There are a few places where you can camp in a spot by yourself. Because of the openess of the campgrounds, this lake is very popular with groups of RV's, 50 at a time.No fees.

Directions   From Interstate 5 about 65 miles north of Sacramento take the Maxwell exit, gowest on Maxwell/Stites Rd to Stites, go left on Stites/Lodoga Road to right at the sign for East Park Reservoir. The gets you onto the southeastern arm of the lake which is less developed and more suitable for paddling.

Resources   Gilmore Peak & Lodoga topo maps from USGS; Mendocino National Forest map from USFS.

Advisory   Watch for power boats.Keep an eye out for rising winds.

Information   East Park Reservoir, 530-968-5267; Bureau Of Reclamation, 530-275-1554

Highland Springs Reservoir

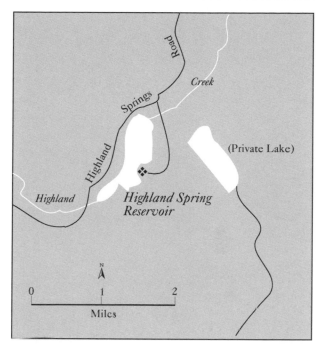

Description Highland Springs Reservoir is a small quiet lake ideal for just floating about with nowhere to go. Partly because there is nowhere to go. Four paddle strokes and you are on the other side of the lake. At 150 surface acres, you're not going to break any distance records, but you might catch a nice nap in a quiet setting. Gas motors are prohibited on Highland Springs.

Camping See Clear Lake, *Camping*, pg. 43

Directions From Highway 29 near Kelseyville, go south on Highland Springs Rd to the Reservoir.

Resources Highland Springs topo map from USGS

Advisory Have a good time.

Information Lake County Flood Control, 707-263-2343

Quiet little Highland Spring Reservoir

Cattails give a home to a plethora of song birds

41

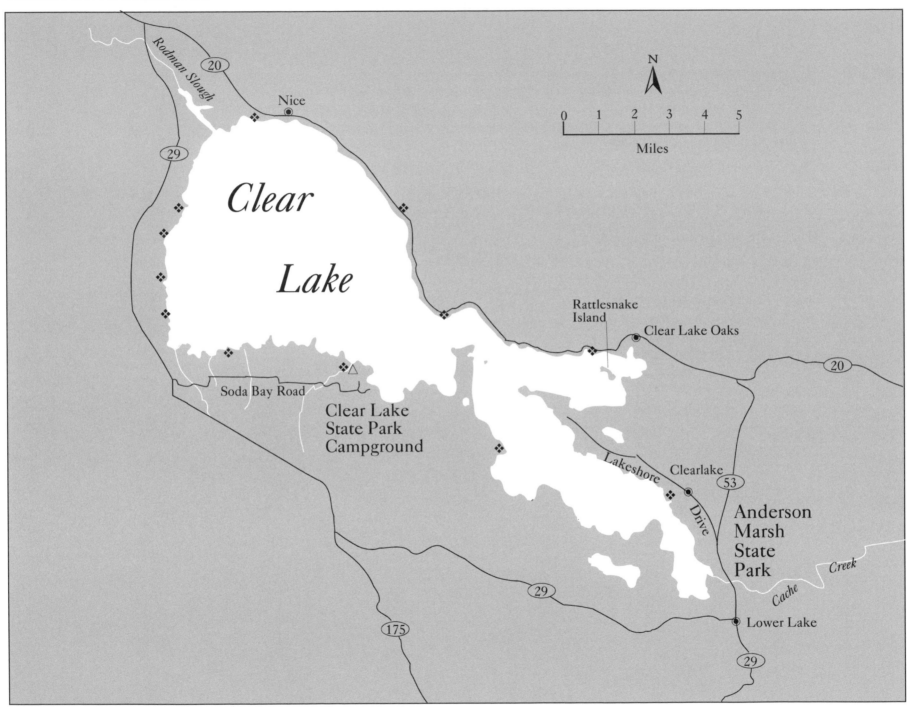

Clear Lake & Anderson Marsh

Description
Clear Lake is large natural lake with 43,000 surface acres and more than 100 miles of shoreline. The lake sits at 1,300 feet at the foot of 4,200 foot Mount Konocti among the pines and oaks with willows dominating the shoreline. At one time Clear Lake was the home to the Pomo and Lile'ek tribes who fed on the plentiful fish and game that lived in and around the lake. The fishing is still good and in spite of massive residential development there is still a lot of wildlife in the area including wood ducks nesting in the trees, herons fishing the shallows, wintering peregrine falcons, golden eagles, great horned owls pond turtles in the creeks and marshes and once in a while you might be able to catch a glimpse of a beaver, bobcat or mink.

There are many coves and inlets along the western shore just below the town of Lakeport and a few islands to explore. However, the best paddling spots on the lake are Rodman Slough at the very north end of the lake and Anderson Marsh Natural Preserve at the very south end.

Camping
Clear lake is a residentially developed area and there is really only one place for camping in a natural setting near the lake. Clear Lake State Park campgroud is right on the lake with 147 sites, running water, flush toilets, showers and tables for a fee; reserve through Destinet (800-283-CAMP); *see also "Camping", Lake Mendocino, previous page.*)

Directions
From Highway 101 take Highway 20 east; from Interstate 5 take Highway 20 west; Highways 20, 29 and 53 encircle the lake; follow the map and signs to get to your chosen destination on Clear lake.

Resources
Upper Lake, Lakeport, Lucerne, Clearlake Oaks, Kelseyville, Clearlake Highlands and Lower Lake topo maps from USGS.

Advisory
There are a lot of power boats and waterskiers on Clear Lake during the vacation season. Keep an eye out for them. Strong winds can make the open water of the lake unsafe for canoeing.

Information
Clear Lake State Park, 707-279-4293

A dormant volcanoe hovers over Clear Lake

Cache Creek flows east along Anderson Marsh

Anderson Marsh at Clear Lakes east end   *Courtesy CDPR*

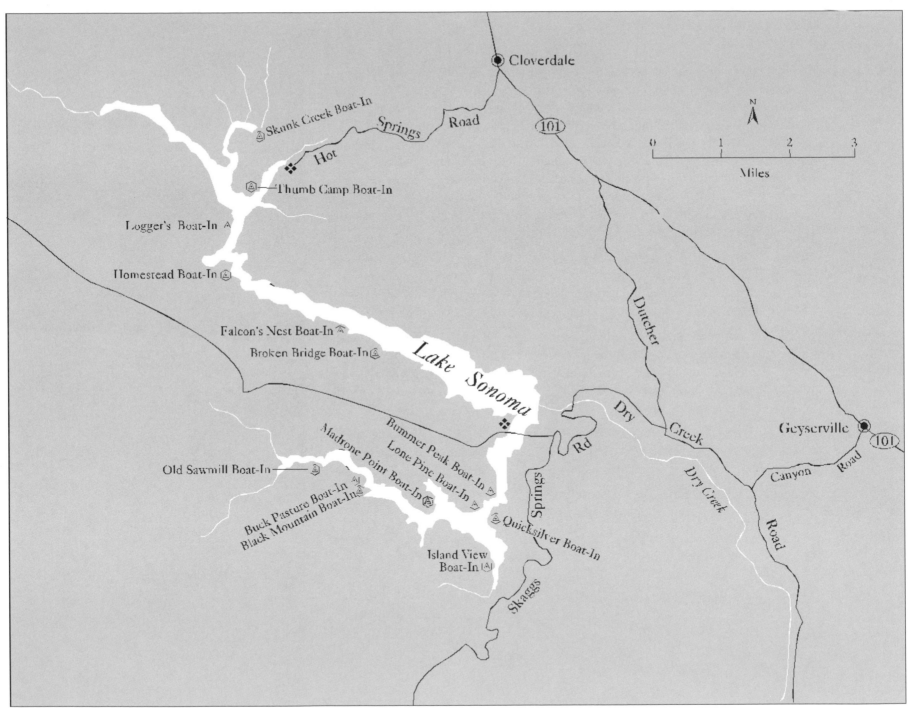

Cloverdale

101

N

0   1   2   3

Miles

Skunk Creek Boat-In

Hot Springs Road

Thumb Camp Boat-In

Logger's Boat-In

Homestead Boat-In

Falcon's Nest Boat-In

Broken Bridge Boat-In

Lake Sonoma

Dutcher

Dry Creek

Geyserville

101

Bummer Peak Boat-In

Lone Pine Boat-In

Old Sawmill Boat-In

Madrone Point Boat-In

Buck Pasture Boat-In

Black Mountain Boat-In

Quicksilver Boat-In

Springs Rd

Dry Creek

Canyon Road

Road

Island View
Boat-In

Skaggs

Lake Sonoma

Description   Lake Sonoma has 2500 surface acres and is set at 451 feet elevation, amid the rounded, oak shaded hills of the coast range. In a way Lake Sonoma is two lakes. One, a large, noisy, power boat infested, recreational lake in the southern end. And, two, a quiet, pastoral, no wake paddler's paradise at the northern end.

Camping   There are 15 boat-in campgrounds offering 115 primitive campsites with portable toilets, tables, fire rings, no water. A permit is required from the Visitor's Center at the dam. Open year round.

Directions   From Highway 101 south of Cloverdale take the Cloverdale Blvd exit, *(most of the available maps show Hot Springs Road coming right off of Cloverdale Blvd, this is no longer the case)*, go north on Cloverdale Blvd till you see the Del Webb development on the west side of the road, turn west onto Del Webb Wy, turn left onto S.Foothill Drive, this turns into Hot Springs Road at the end of the cul du sac, stay on windy Hot Springs Road to the Yorty Creek Day Use Area. You can park here overnight while you paddle-in to the campsites.

Resources   Cloverdale, Warm Springs Dam and Geyserville topo maps from the USGS. Brochure from the Lake Sonoma Recreation Area, *(see information below)*.http://www.spn.usace.army.mil/lakesonoma/Lake%20Sonoma2.htm

Advisory   Bring your own water to the boat-in camps. Watch for power boats in the lower end of the lake.

Information   Lake Sonoma Recreation Area 707-433-9483

The front end of Lake Sonoma, near the dam

The back end of Lake Sonoma, no power boat wakes

Larry "The Supply Guy" on his way to the paddle-in camp

Lake Berryessa is huge, perfect for long distance paddling

Exploring coves and creeks uncovers many natural treasures

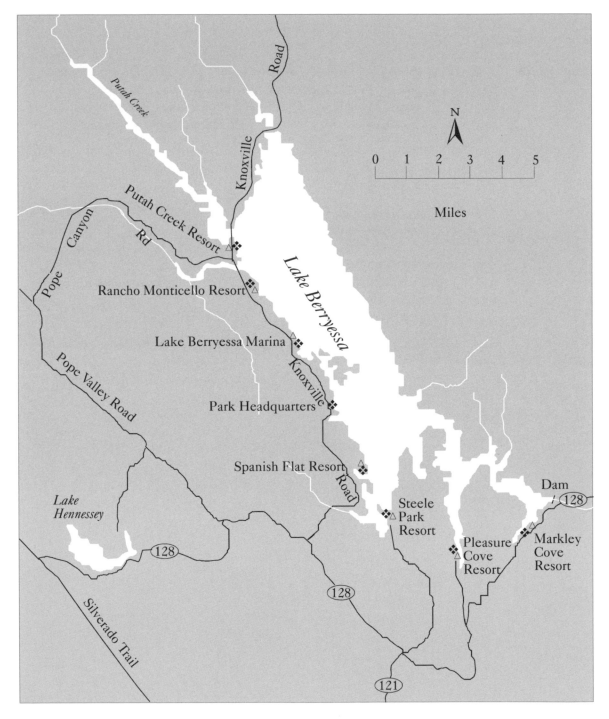

Lake Berryessa

Description Lake Berryessa is a huge, popular recreational lake. It has 13,000 surface acres lots of power boats, and during the summer the place is a sweltering hot spot. However, it still has a great deal to offer the paddler. At the south and north ends of the lake are coves and feeder streams to explore. On the west shore are several islands. In the winter and spring the surrounding hills are green, the weather can be very pleasant and the cold water deters the water skiers and their power boats.

Camping All the camping around Lake Berryessa is resort style with tents mixed with full hookup motor homes, picnic tables, restrooms, showers, snack bars, restuarants, etc, for a fee. Call to make a reservation; Rancho Monticello Resort, 707-966-2188; Putah Creek Park, 707-966-2116; Lake Berryessa Resort, 707-966-2161; Markley Cove Resort, 707-966-2134; Pleasure Cove Resort, 707-966-2172; Spanish Flat Resort, 707-966-7700; Steele Park Resort, 707-966-2123

Directions From Highway 128 east of Napa go north on Berryessa/Knoxville Road

Resources Walter Springs, Brooks, Chiles Vale, Lake Berryessa, Montecello Dam, Capel Valley & Mount Vaca topo maps from USGS.

Advisory Watch for power boats and high winds.

Information Bureau Of Reclamation, 707-966-2111; Lake Berryessa Chamber of Commerce, 800-726-1256

One of Lake Berryessa's explorable feeder creek

There are several islands to explore on Lake Berryessa

Up Putah Creek at sunset

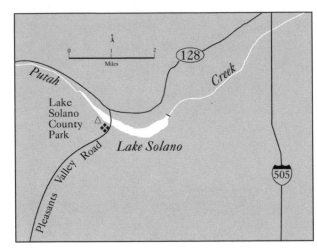

Lake Solano

Description   Lake Solano is an ideal paddle spot. Considering its proximity to civilization, Lake Solano is relatively quiet. It's not really a lake as much as it is a creek (Putah Creek) with a small dam on it. It is thin and about 2.5 miles long. Most of the crowds go to nearby Lake Berryessa. Power boats are prohibited. Lake Solano is the afterbay for Monticello Dam on Lake Berryessa so the water stays pretty cold (about 50 degrees) as it comes out of the bottom of the dam.

Camping   There are 67 sites for tents or RV with piped water, flush toilets, picnic tables, fire grills, showers and a store, for a fee, no reservations.

Directions   From Highway 128 east of Lake Berryessa and west of the town of Winters turn south on Pleasan Valley Road, continue on to Lake Solano County Park.

Resources   Monticello Dam topo map from USGS.

Advisory   You could get so relaxed that you fall asleep and wake up with a sunburn.

Information   Lake Solano County Park, 916-795-2990

Intimate Lake Solano on Putah Creek

Spring Lake

Description   Spring Lake is a very small (75 surface acres within a 350 acre park), pleasant lake. Its big advantage is the available camping near a major population center, Santa Rosa. Spring Lake is a floater, you float around and enjoy the scenery, maybe have a picnic. Gas motors are prohibited.

Camping   Spring Lake Regional Park has 4 sites for tents only and 30 sites for tents and motor homes with piped water, picnic tables, restrooms, showers and fire grills for a fee; reservations recommended.

Directions   From US 101 in Santa Rosa take the Highway 12 East/Sonoma exit, when the freeway ends go straight at the light onto Hoen Avenue, go about 2 mile to left on Newanga Avenue to the lake.

Resources   Santa Rosa topo map from USGS.

Advisory   Have a good time.

Information   Spring Lake Regional Park, 707-966-2116

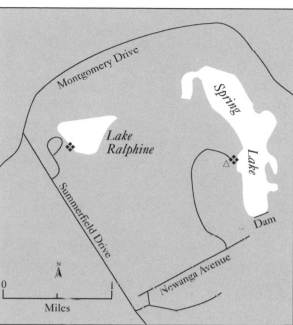

Spring Lake is a welcome relief from the sprawl of Santa Rosa

Tiny Lake Ralphine is good for a float and a nap

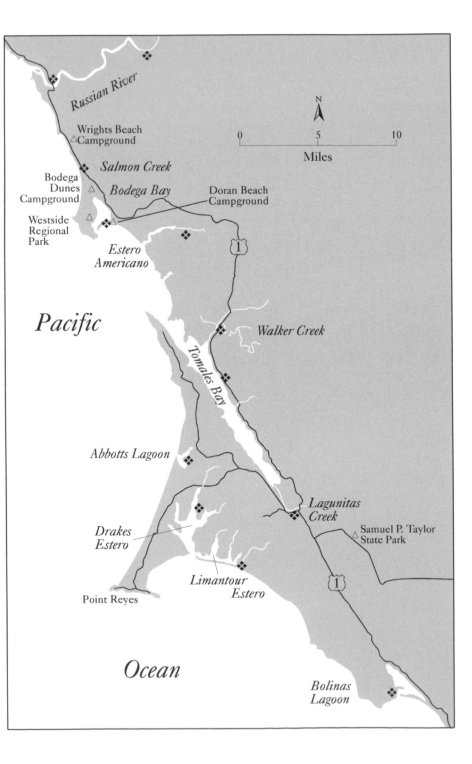

The Sonoma/Marin Coast

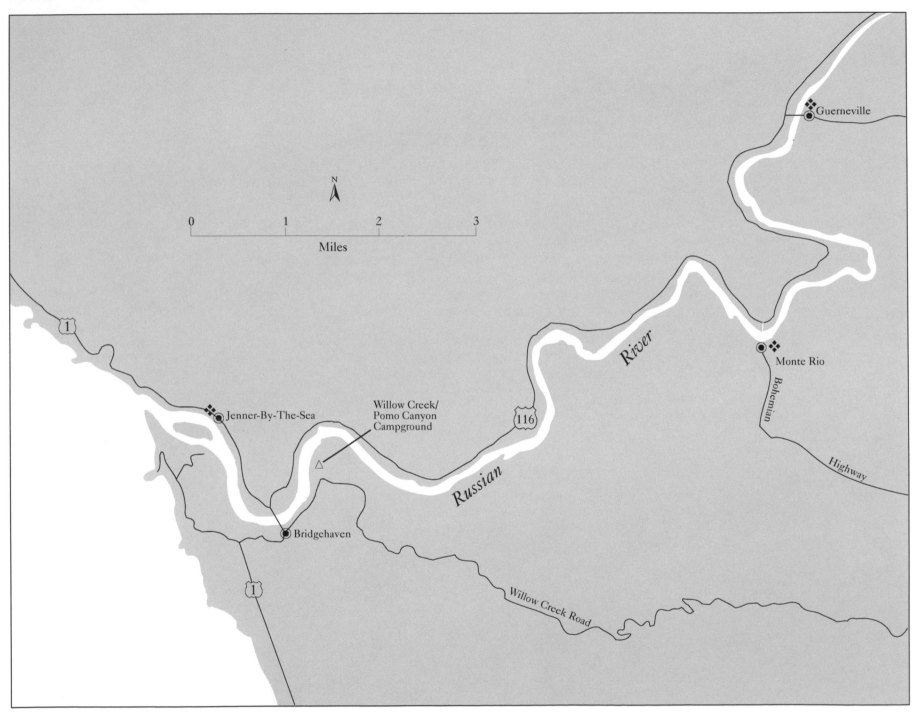

Russian River

Description You can paddle around at the mouth of the Russian River and explore Penny Island. Where the river empties into the ocean is very dangerous. Paddlers have been swept out to sea. Due to the amount of water the Russian River usually carries, upstream paddling is strenuous. The Russian River is considered to be more of a class I paddle. Most paddlers start up river at Monte Rio or Guernville, paddle down to the river mouth and then shuttle back to their cars. It's about 15 miles from Guernville to the sea wtih two small dams to portage around.

Camping The nearest natural setting to camp in is the Willow Creek/Pomo Canyon Campgrounds. There are 21 environmental campsites set in a redwood grove with toilets, fireplaces and tables. You have to bring your own water. From the south side of the bridge over the Russian River go east off Hwy 1 on Willow Creek Road for about a mile to the campground parking lot on the north side of the road. Campers must check in at Bodega Dunes Campground; call 707-875-3483. See also; Bodega Dunes campground at Bodega Bay Harbor, page 55.

Directions Right along Hwy 1 at Jenner By-The-Sea. Put-in at the public boat ramp at the Jenner Visitors Center just inland from the mouth of the river on the north bank off Hwy 1. You can put in at the Willow/Pomo campground if you are staying there. To take the trip down river, you can put in at either Guernville or Monte Rio off of Highway 116. There are several places that rent kayaks and canoes and provide shuttles.

Resources Duncan Mills, Camp Meeker, Guerneville and Healdsberg topo maps from USGS

Advisory You should have some paddling experience before heading out on a moving water excursion. Winter and Spring flows can be heavy with flood stage being reached every few years. This higher water volume makes upstream paddling almost impossible. Don't paddle this or any river at flood stage. The current where the river meets the ocean is very strong most of the year. Paddlers have been swept out to sea here. On shore winds make the down river trip very chilly and strenuous.

Information Jenner Visitors Center; 707-875-3483

Mouth of the Russian River from above   *Courtesy CDPR*

Russian River meets the sea

Upstream on the Russian River

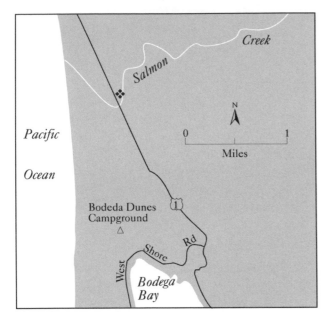

Salmon Creek

Description   Paddling Salmon Creek is one of those magical experiences that leaves you with a true sense of wonder. It's a very short paddle, maybe a half a mile out to the ocean and three quarters of a mile inland for the highway. Within this small area are several distinct wetland habitats: near the mouth of the creek are saltwater and brackish marshes and upstream are freshwater marshes. Wildlife abounds, especially waterfowl. This is heaven for bird watchers.

Camping   See *Bodega Bay, Camping*, next page.

Directions   Right off Highway 101 just north of Bodega Bay.

Resources   Bodega Head topo map from USGS

Advisory   During winter and spring rains, river flows can make upstream travel difficult to impossible, and currents can be tricky where the creek meets the ocean. This is an environmentally sensative area; tread lightly and quietly.

Information   None

An intimate paddle awaits you inland on Salmon Creek

Salmon Creek meets the ocean

Bodega Bay & Harbor

Description   Bodega Bay is a well protected harbor with marshlands along the southern arm of the bay. This is one of the more developed paddling spots on the coast. Bodega Bay is still a thriving commercial and recreational fishing harbor. Away from the bustle of the harbor to the north, the southern marshland and tidal mud flats have a plethora of common and uncommon sea birds to observe.. Alfred Hitchcock's movie *The Birds* was filmed in the town of Bodega (I'm pretty sure it's fiction).

Camping   Bodega Dunes is a beautiful beachside campground. There are 98 campsites with flush toilets, tables, fireplaces, water and showers for a fee; reservations thru Mistix, *(see Resources, page)*. Call the Sonoma Coast State Beach at 707-875-3483. Doran Beach Regional Park sits right on the beach of Bodega Bay. There are 138 campsites including 10 sites for tents only with flush toilets, tables, fireplaces, water and showers for a fee; no reservations. For info call the County Parks Department at 707-875-3540.

Directions   Right off Hwy 1 just north of Tomales Bay. There are several free public boat ramps available around Bodega Bay.

Resources   Bodega Head topo map from the USGS

Advisory   The open water away from shore is not recommended for open canoes unless the wind and water are calm. Keep an eye on the tide and wind. Watch for fishing boats.

Information   Bodega Bay Harbor; 707-875-3422

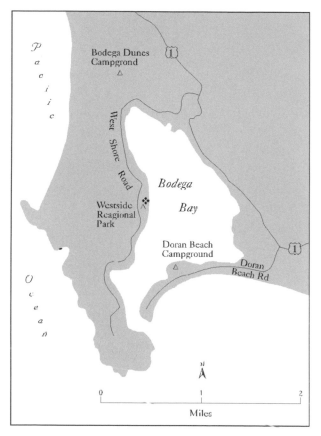

Sea birds feed in great numbers in the mud flats of Bodega Bay

Bodega Harbor still has a bustling fishing trade

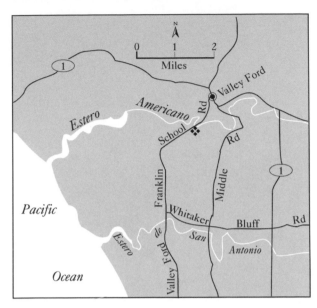

Paddling doesn't get any more intimate than this

The put-in on Estero Americano

Estero Americano

Description   Estero Americano lies in a "drowned valley" along Americano Creek. A drowned valley is caused by a rise in ocean level due to prehistoric glacial melting. This is one of my favorite paddling destinations in all of California. At the put in, Estero Americano is barely 30 feet wide. As you start out towards the ocean it meanders back and forth throught rolling pasture lands. After about 3 miles it widens out to almost a 1/2 mile wide. It's crucial to paddle the estero at high tide. At low tide you can only paddle the first 3 miles and then the water gets too shallow to continue to the ocean.

There is ample wildlife to view, especially out near the sea, including: tule elk, birds of prey, wading birds and white pelicans. The hills stay green most of the year and in spring they get a carpet of yellow flowers.

Camping   See *Bodega Bay, Camping*, previous page.

Directions   From Highway 1, south of Bodega, in the town of Valley Ford, at Dinnucci's Italian Diner go south on Valley Ford Estero/Franklin School Road until you come to the bridge across the estero. Park on the south side of the bridge and put in.

Resources   Valley Ford topo map from USGS

Advisory   Low tide can strand you miles from the put-in. High winds can make the journey out towards the ocean difficult and sometimes dangerous.

Information   None

Walker Creek

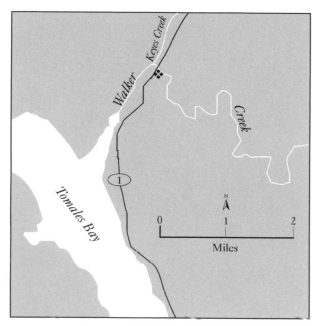

Description   Walker Creek and its tributary Keys Creek feed into the north end of Tomales Bay. It's a sweet little paddle about three miles long. Where the creek empties into Tomales Bay is the Walker Creek delta with over 100 acres of salt marsh and mud flats (don't get stranded at low tide). Many species of birds feed in the delta, including: whimbrels, short-billed dowitchers and long-billed curlews. You can paddle out into Tomales Bay and paddle around Hog Island,

Camping   See *Tomales Bay, Camping*, next page.

Directions   Just north of Tomales Bay where Highway 1 turns east away from the bay, go about 2 miles along Walker Creek to the where Highway 1 crosses the creek, park and put in.

Resources   Tomales topo map from USGS.

Advisory   Keep an eye on the tides and don't get stuck in the mud flats. You can get further up the creek at high tide. If you venture out onto Tomales Bay, watch for high winds and don't go anywhere near the mouth of the bay. There are very dangerous currents there.

Information   Tomales Bay State Park: 415-669-1140

Walker Creek is an intimate paddle in a riparian corridor

57

The south end of Tomales Bay

Tomales Bay State Park

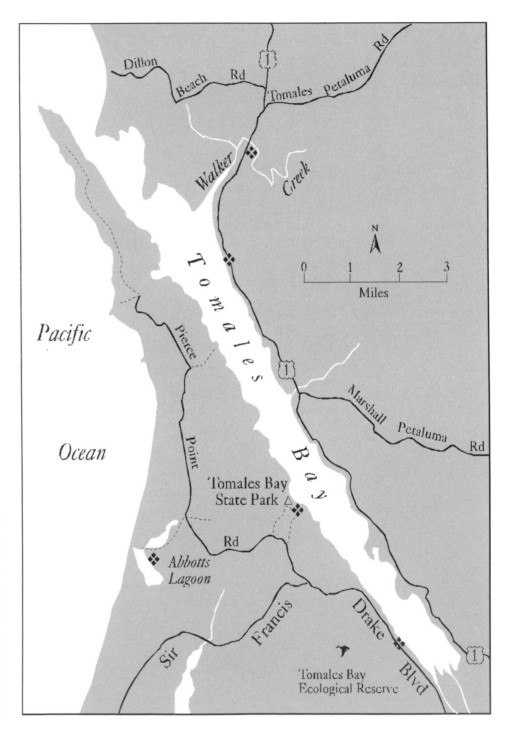

Tomales Bay

Tomales Bay offers long distance paddling   *Courtesy CDPR*

Description Tomales Bay was created by the movement of the San Andreas Fault which runs directly under the bay. The bay is 10 miles long and 3/4 mile wide. Although you can drive to the campground at Tomales State Park it's more fun to park in one of the towns and paddle in to the Tomales Bay State Park for an overnight stay. Be sure to call ahead to make sure a campsite is available before you paddle all the way across the bay with your camping gear. Tomales Bay has a real feel for being on the ocean water. The western shore of the bay makes for some good exploring. Nearby Point Reyes National Seashore offers many hiking opportunities.

Camping Tomales Bay State Park is on Tomales Bay just off Pierce Point Rd on the northeastern side of Point Reyes National Seashore. There are just 6 campsites for tents only with water, flush toilets and a fire ring for a fee; no reservations. This is supposed to be a campground for bicyclists and no vehicles are allowed in the park after closing. You have to park your car outside the park at night and hike in for one mile to the campground. Samuel P. Taylor Park is just off Sir Francis Drake Blvd east of Hwy 1 and west of San Rafael. There are 60 campsites, 25 for tents only, with water, flush toilets, tables, fireplaces, food lockers and showers for a fee; reserve through Destinet (800-283-CAMP).

Directions Along Hwy 1 south of Bodega Bay.

Resources Tomales, Point Reyes NE and Inverness topo maps from the USGS.

Advisory The open water away from shore is not recommended for open canoes unless the wind and water are calm. Keep an eye on the tide and winds. Where the bay meet the ocean there are very dangerous tidal currents.

Information Tomales Bay State Park: 415-669-1140

Unusually calm water on the bay

Wildlife abounds in and around Tomales Bay

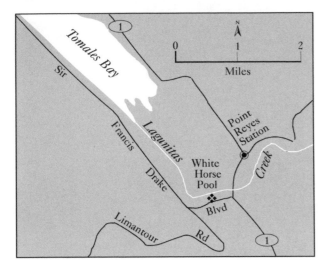

Lagunitas/Papermill Creek

Description Papermill Creek is also known a Lagunitas Creek. It is the largest of the creeks that feed into Tomales Bay. The paddleable part is at the south end of Tomales Bay for about 2 miles. This riparian corridor is reputed to have great fishing.The largest Silver Salmon ever caught in California (22 pounds) was caught here in 1959.

Camping See *Tomales Bay, Camping*, previous page.

Directions From Highway 1 at the south end of the town of Point Reyes Station, turn west on Sir Francis Drake Blvd., just a short ways down the road look on the right (north) for White House Pool "fishing access". That's the put in.

Resources Inverness topo map from USGS.

Advisory Keep an eye on the tides. If you enter Tomales Bay be very careful not to get stranded on the mud flat at the southern end of the bay at low tide.

Information Tomales Bay State Park: 415-669-1140

Lagunitas Greek from the White House Pool

Looking east on Papermill Creek

60

Abbotts Lagoon

Description   Abbotts Lagoon lies within the boundries of Point Reyes National Seashore. This little lagoon has about three miles of shoreline which rises and falls with the tide. There is a natural dam that separates the two parts of the lagoon and there is a portage of several hundred feet from the parking lot.

Camping   Point Reyes Hostel is in Point Reyes National Seashore off Limantour Road. There are beds available with water, flush toilets and showers for a fee. Check in time is 4:30 to 9:00pm with a curfew of 11:00pm. Reservations advised for groups larger than five. Tomales Bay State Park *(see Tomales Bay, previous page)*, Samuel P. Taylor State Park *(see Tomales Bay, previous page)*.

Directions   From Hwy 1 just north of the town of Olema take Sir Francis Drake Blvd. northwest into Point Reyes National Seashore, go north on Pierce Road to the Abbotts Lagoon parking lot on the west side of the road.

Resources   Drakes Bay topo map from the USGS, *Point Reyes* by Dorothy Whitman.

Advisory   Keep an eye on the wind and tides. Very high tides can breach the beach between the lagoon and the oceans making for some tricky currents in the inlet.

Information   Point Reyes National Seashore: 415-663-1092

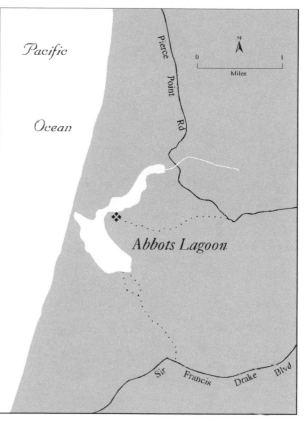

The northern end of Abbotts Lagoon

The Oyster Farm put in on Drakes Estero

Channel exploration on Drakes Estero

Scotch Broom blooming on a bluff above Drakes Estero

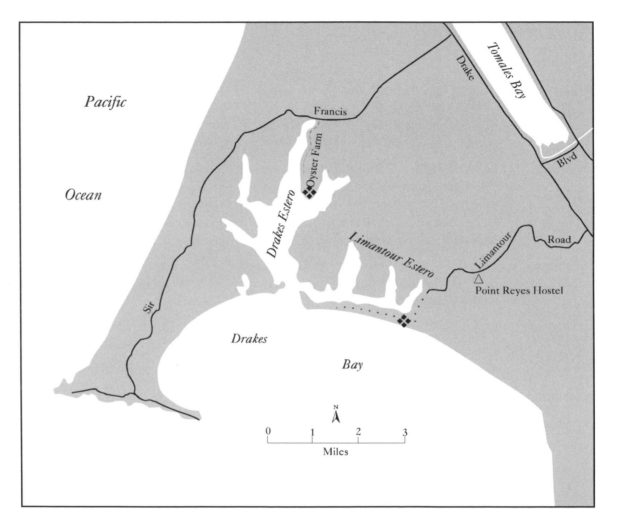

Drakes & Limantour Esteros

Description Drake's Estero and Limantour Estero Reserve lie within the boundaries of Point Reyes National Seashore in Drake's Bay. This is the place where Sir Francis Drake supposedly landed to repair his ship the Golden Hinde in 1579. This is a large estuarine environment with many fingers to explore. The tidal mud flats and salt marshes in the area are home to a wide variety of birds, animals and plant life. Opportunites for photographing and observing wildlife abound.

Camping Point Reyes Hostel *(see Abbotts Lagoon, page 61)*, Tomales Bay State Park *(see Tomales Bay, page 59)*, Samuel P. Taylor State Park *(see Tomales Bay, page 59)*.

Directions To put in on Drakes Estero, from Hwy 1 at Point Reyes Station take Sir Francis Drake Blvd. west until it crosses the estero at it's northern most point where you can put in at high tide. To put in on Limantour Estero, from Hwy 1 at Point Reyes Station take Sir Francis Drake Blvd. west, go left at Limantour Rd. to the estero.

Resources Drakes Bay topo map from the USGS, *Point Reyes* by Dorothy Whitman.

Advisory Keep an eye on the tide and winds. Where the estero meets the ocean there are very dangerous currents. Limantour Estero Reserve is closed to all boating during seal pupping season, March 15th thru June 30th.

Information Point Reyes National Seashore: 415-663-1092

Cattails on Limantour Estero

Limantour Estero at low tide

There are many channels to explore on Limantour Estero

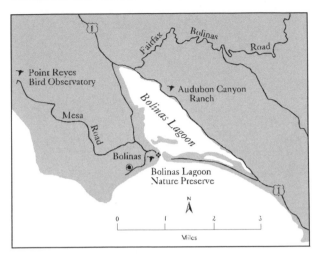

Bolinas Lagoon from Mount Tamalpais's back side

Egrets feeding in the shallows of Bolinas Lagoon

Bolinas Lagoon

Description   Although the residents of the town of Bolinas wish the town were invisible to visitors, it remains one of the most beautifully unique communities in California. Bolinas Lagoon is a small tidal pool just off Hwy 1 and like Tomales Bay, this body of water was created by the San Andreas Fault which runs directly below it. There are four wildlife reserves in the area: Bolinas Lagoon Nature Reserve, Audubon Canyon Ranch, Duxbury Reef Marine Reserve, and Point Reyes Bird Observatory. Subsequently, there is an abundance of wildlife to be seen here including osprey, gulls, diving ducks, great blue herons, snowy egrets and great egrets. The elaborate courtship dances of the egrets and herons can be seen at the Aububon Canyon Ranch in January and Bolinas Lagoons salt marshes are a favorite feeding ground for all of these birds. Nearby John Muir Woods provides some day hiking thru one of California's most beautiful redwood forests.

Camping   Samuel P. Taylor State Park *(see Tomales Bay, page 59).*

Directions   Right off Hwy 1 at Bolinas. Park and put-in at the mouth of the lagoon.

Resources   Bolinas topo map from USGS

Advisory   Keep an eye on the tide; currents can be tricky at the mouth of the lagoon. On shore winds can make the trip cold and strenuous.

Information   Marin Audubon Society: 415-969-9244

The Central Coast

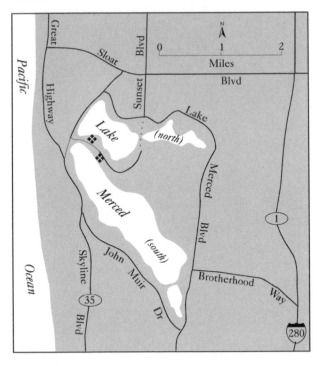

Lake Merced

Description   Lake Merced used to be a tidal lagoon until a barrierbeach closed it off from the sea, turning it into a freshwater lake. This lake is less than a mile from the house where I grew up. It's actually three lakes with a road, a parking lot and Harding Municipal Golf Course between them. The north lake is prettier and more natural. It has two sections with a narrow pass between them (perfect for paddle boats. North Lake Merced is surrounded by tules which give home to song birds and muskrats. There is a picnic area and fishing beach. South Lake Merced is more open with some rip-rap shoreline. There is a boat house with a restuarant and a bar that rents row boats. Gas motors are prohibited on both sections of the lake.

Camping   This is the middle of San Francisco. Ain't no campin' here. Try a motel.

Directions   Going south on Highway 101/1 about one quarter mile south of the Golden Gate Bridge toll plaza, take the 19th Avenue exit, go straight on Park Presidio, you'll weave through Golden "Gate Park and come out on 19th Avenue, stay on 19th Avenue for a few miles then turn right (west) on Sloat Boulevard, go a couple of miles then turn left (south) onto Skyline Boulevard, the entrance to Lake Merced/ Harding Golf Course is on the left. Put in where you can. From the south on Interstate 280, take 19th Avenue at the end of the freeway to the left (west) onto Sloat Boulevard...to Skyline Boulevard...

Resources   San Francisco South topo map from USGS.

Advisory   Watch for strong winds. Don't get in the path of the scullers (rowboats) who have a club and practice on the south section of the lake.

Information   San Francisco Parks & Recreation Department, 415-831-2773, Lake Merced Boat House, 415-753-1101

Lake Merced South

Lake Merced North

Pescadero Marsh

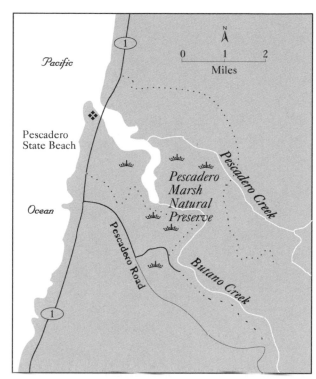

Description Pescadero Marsh Natural Preserve is a 510 acre protected wildlife sanctuary. This is a small area, but packed with wildlife viewing opportunities in the fall and winter. The marsh is closed to paddling in the spring and summer to protect all the animals during their breeding season.

Camping Butano State Park has 21 sites for tents or motor homes and 18 walk-in sites with piped water, tables, fire grills and flush toilets for a fee, reserve thru Destinet 800-444-7275 for a fee.

Directions Right off Highway 1 south of Half Moon Bay.

Resources San Gregorio and Pigeon Point topo maps from USGS; various pamphlets available from the Pescadero Marsh Natural Preserve including a bird watching checklist with more than 200 species on it.

Advisory Pescadero Marsh Natural Preserve is closed to paddling from March 15 to September 1 for the breeding season. This in an incredibly fragile environment with many endangered species of birds, mammals, reptiles and plants. Be quiet and give the animals lots of room. Don't go in large groups and if you see someone else is already paddling there, you might want to think about going someplace else. It is quite a priviledge that we can still paddle this exquisite wild place. Let's enjoy it blissfully and care for it impeccably at the same time.

Information Pescadero Marsh Natural Preserve, 415-879-2170

Beautiful and fragile Pescadero Marsh   *Courtesy CDPR*

69

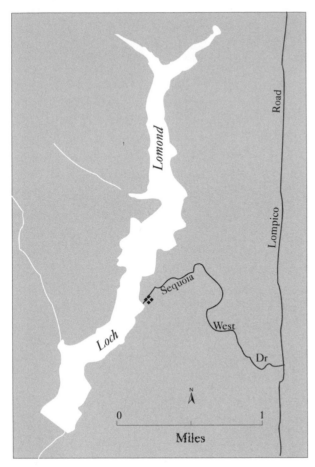

Loch Lomond

Description   Loch Lomond is a gorgeous little lake. At 3 1/2 miles long you can definately get some strokes in on this lake. The shore is lined with coastal redwoods making this one of the prettiest paddles around. Damned up on Newell Creek, Lock Lomond is a drinking water source for the city of Santa Cruz, so gas motors and body contact with the water are prohibited.

Camping   Big Basin Redwoods State Park has 107 sites for tent or motorhome, 38 walk-in sites, 35 tent cabins and 10 backpack sites with piped water tables, fire grills, flush toilets, coin-operated showers and a grocery store for a fee, reserve thru Destinet 800-444-7275 for a fee; Henry Cowell Redwoods State Park has 112 sites for tents or motor homes with piped water, tables, flush toilets, fire grills and coin operated showers for a fee.

Directions   From Highway 1 in Santa Cruz take Highway 9 north to the town of Ben Lomond, from there turn east at the intersection of the sign for Loch Lomond and follow the signs to the lake.

Resources   Felton topo map from USGS; pamphlet from the Loch Lomond Recreation Area.

Advisory   The lake is only open during the spring and summer from dawn to dusk. There are lots of rules and regulations here at Loch Lomond. The pamphlet you get at the gate lists them all. You must get off the water one hour before the park closes.

Information   Loch Lomond Recreation Area, 831-4205320

Coastal Redwoods line the shores of Loch Lomond

Pinto Lake

Description Pinto Lake is a small recreational lake used mostly by shoreline fisherman. There is a strictly enforced speed limit on the lake. They'll call the cops if you even make a wake. I don't think any paddlers have ever gotten a ticket, but "Hey buddy, you wanna slow down them paddle strokes." The northern end of the lake in the fingers is the best paddling with lots of shorebirds, song birds and water fowl feeding in the tules.

Camping If you have a motor home or a trailer you can camp right at the lake. However the "camping" area is not all that scenic. See *Loch Lomond: Camping, page 70;* see also *Elkhorn Slough: Camping, page 74;* see also *Big Sur River: Camping, page 77.*

Directions From Highway 1 in Watsonville take the Highway 152 exit, go left on Green Valley Road, go about 2 1/2 miles to a left into Pinto Lake County Park.

Resources Watsonville West topo map from USGS.

Advisory None.

Information Pinto Lake County Park, 831-722-8129

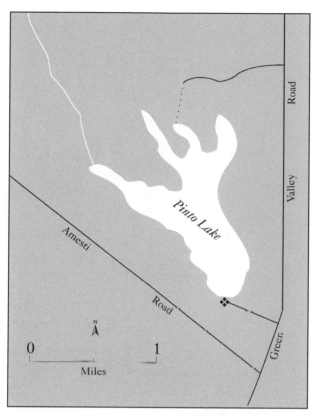

Ducks feed in the tules of Pinto Lake

During a flood year you can paddle all over the valley

Wouldn't you like to live here?

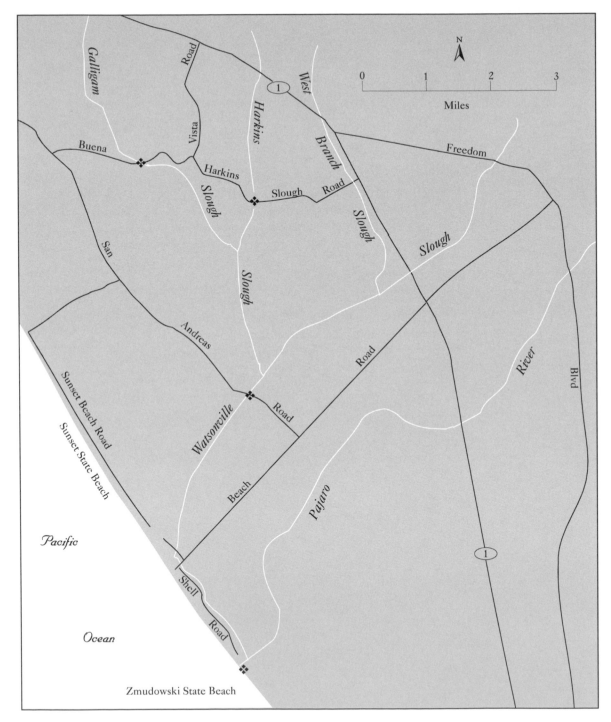

Pajaro Valley Wetlands

The Pajaro River meet the mighty Pacific Ocean

Description Welcom to Watsonville, the artichoke capitol of the world. The Pajaro Valley wetlands is an area of 21 square miles of freshwater marshes, sloughs and artichoke fields, which includes the Pajaro River and Watsonville, Harkins, Sturve, Galligan and Hanson Sloughs. The upstream area, especially near Harkins Slough, is still in its natural state. A lot of the sloughs have been channelized for agricultual use. It is still a great place to paddle. The problem is access is limited to impossible. When I was there it was a flood year and I got onto the water off Harkins Slough Road. There was a gate across the road with a sign "flooded". I parked off the road carried my kayak down to 6 inches of water going across the road and had one of the best paddles of my life. I was probably paddling across private property and I do apologize. The Pajaro River is a class I paddle through fields of artichokes. I never did find access to the Pajaro River.

I put this area in the book because I found it to be a fabulous place to paddle. I will return here and in future editions of this book I hope to have reliable put in information. The put ins marked on the map are guesses on my part of likely access points. You can try them, but don't trespass on private property. If nothing else check out the annual Artichoke Festival. You haven't lived till you've tasted artichoke ice cream.

Camping See *Elkhorn Slough: Camping, page* 74; see also *Big Sur River: Camping, page 77*.

Directions South of Highway 1 in Watsonville.

Resources Watsonville West, Watsonville East and Moss Landing topo maps from USGS.

Advisory The area surrounding the Watsonville Slough and the Pajaro River is mostly privately owned land. Legal put-ins are hard to find. Respect people's privacy and don't trespass on private land. You can get busted and that would pretty much ruin your trip.

Information This book is about it.

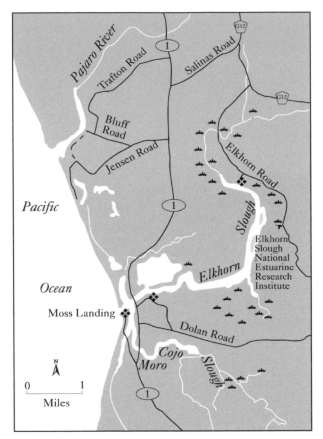

Wildlife abounds in the backwaters of Elkhorn Slough

Elkhorn Slough

Description   Elkhorn Slough flows among coastal live oak and Monterey pines and empties into Monterey Bay. This estuarine eco-system of sloughs, creeks and salt water marshes is home to an incredible diversity of birds and other wildlife including: red-shouldered hawks, ruddy turnstones, hummingbirds, common loons, acorn woodpeckers, brown pelicans, and even the occasional small Smoothhound or Leopard sharks feeding in it's deeper waters. Be sure to visit the Elkhorn Slough National Estuarine Research Reserve.

Camping   Henry Cowell Redwoods State Park has 112 campsites with water, flush toilets, showers, tables and fireplaces for a fee, reserve thru Destinet 800-444-7275; Sunset State Beach campground has 90 sites with running water, flush toilets, fireplaces, tables and showers for a fee, reserve thru Destinet 800-444-7275 for a fee; Andrew Molera State Park campground has several walk-in camps with running water, toilets, fireplaces and tables for a fee, no reservations; Bottcher's Gap campground has 20 sites,(nine for tent only), with running water, toilets, fireplaces and tables for a fee; no reservations; Fremont Peak State Park has 25 primitive sites with piped water, tables, vault toilets and fire rings for a fee, no reservations.

Directions   North of Moss Landing on Hwy 1 take Dolan Road east 3.5 miles to Elkhorn Road, go north past the Reserve entrance 3 miles to Kirby Park. There is also a public boat ramp near the mouth of the Elkhorn Slough at Moss Landing Harbor just off Hwy 1 about a quarter mile north of where the highway crosses the slough.

Resources   Moss Landing and Prundale USGS topo maps; excellent brochure from the Elkhorn Slough Foundation, *(see below)*.

Advisory   Peak tidal currents under Hyw 1 are dangerous. Keep an eye on the tide. After-noon on-shore winds can make the trip cold and strenuous. Stay back 50 feet from beached harbor seals and sea otters. Respect private lands and leave your boat only at designated areas.

Information   Elkhorn Slough National Estuarine Research Reserve, 408-728-2822; Elkhorn Slough Foundation, 408-728-5939

Salinas River

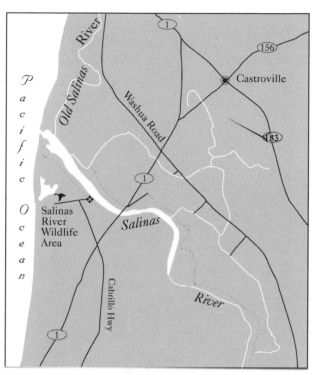

Description The Salinas River used to flow into Elkhorn Slough, but farmers changed its course to open up more farm land. You can paddle severa miles upstream on the river. This portion of the river near the mouth is home to a wide variety of wildlife including snowy plover and endangered brown pelican. Avocets, stilts and gadwalls nest on the islands near the mouth of the river.

After the spring rains have made their way to the sea, a barrier dune will form, cutting the river off from the sea. The mouth of the Salinas River is more like a lake at this point and ideal for paddling.

Camping See *Elkhorn Slough: Camping, previous page.*

Directions From Highway 1 north of Monterey take the Del Monte Boulevard exit, go north on Neponset Road to the Salinas River Wildlife Area.

Resources Moss Landing, Marina and Salinas topo maps from USGS.

Advisory Like all rivers, the Salinas River can run very high in heavy rain years. Check out conditions and don't paddle unless you are sure your skill level is up to the task. There is lots of private property around here. Respect other people's privacy and don't trespass.

Information Salinas River Wildlife Area, 408-649-2870

The Salinas River gets cut off from the sea *Courtesy CDPR*

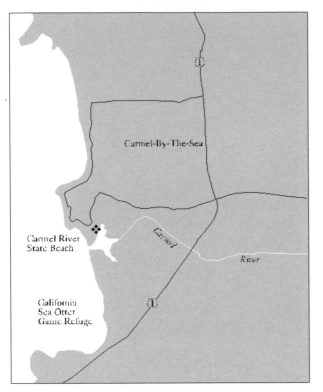

Carmel River Mouth

Description Just off the coast where the Carmel River empties into the Pacific Ocean lies part of the California Sea Otter Game Refuge. Just inland is the Carmel River State Beach and the Carmel River Lagoon & Wetlands Natural Preserve The preserve is a brackish lagoon.

Camping See *Elkhorn Slough: Camping, page* 74; see also *Big Sur River: Camping, next page*.

Directions From Hwy 1 in Carmel-by-the-Sea go west on Rio Road to Santa Lucia Street, go left on Santa Lucia to Carmelo Street, go left on Carmelo to the parking area. Put-in where the river meets the beach.

Resources Monterey and Seaside topo maps from the USGS.

Advisory Keep an eye on the tide; currents can be tricky. On shore winds can make the trip back down river cold and strenuous.

Information California Department of Parks & Recreation: 408-624-4909

The Carmel River becomes a brackish lagoon   *Courtesy CDPR*

Big Sur River

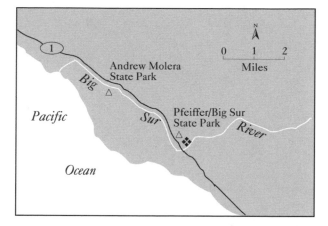

Description The Big Sur River is actually more of a seasonal stream, but it makes for one of the sweetest paddles in California. It's a class I run through the southernmost stand of coastal redwoods. The run is about seven miles from Pfeiffer/Big Sur State Park to Andrew Molera State Park. If you get there too late in the season for kayaks and canoes, use an innertube.

Camping Pfeiffer/Bir Sur State Park has 218 sites with water, fire grills, tables, flush toilets, showers, a laundromat and a store for a fee; Andrew Molera State Park campground has several walk-in camps with running water, toilets, fireplaces and tables for a fee, no reservations; see also *Elkhorn Slough: Camping page* 74.

Directions Right off Highway 1 just south of the town of Big Sur. Put-in at Pfeiffer/Big Sur State Park, take out at Andrew

Resources Big Sur, Pfeiffer Point and Ventana Cones topo maps from USGS

Advisory The Big Sur River can get enough water in it to be dangerours. Check the conditions and use common sense. The river has a very short paddling season, usually in early spring just after the rains.

Information Pfeiffer/Big Sur State Park, 831-667-2315 or Andrcw Molcra Statc Parkm 831-667-2886.

The Big Sur River meets the sea   *Courtesy CDPR*

The Big Sur River is a short, sweet class I paddle   *Courtesy CDPR*

77

Suggested Reading

Paddling Skills

Canoeing: A Trailside Guide ~ by Gordon Grant: A great color book on canoeing basics: choosing a canoe and paddle, canoe design, tandem and solo paddle strokes...very thorough with beautiful photographs and clear illustrations.

Outdoor Pursuits Series: Canoeing ~ by Laurie Gullion: Another great color book on the basics of canoeing with an outstanding section on warm up exercises for paddling. There is a bonus section on some world wide paddling destination.

Maps

National Forest Maps ~ Published by the United States Forest Service (USFS): Indispensible resource! These maps have the most current information of any maps available, especially road type (paved, dirt, gravel, 4 wheel drive, trails, etc.). I would suggest getting all the National Forest maps listed in this book. They're very useful and they're fun to play with. They are available through the U.S. Forest Service, 630 Sansome St., San Francisco, CA 94111: 415-705-2874.

US Geological Survey Maps ~ Published by the United States Geological Survey (USGS): These are the most detailed maps you can get of any area. They show everything, although, some are a little out of date on new roads and housing developments. You can get an index of California's topographical maps by calling the USGS Branch Of Distribution in Denver, Colorado at 303-236-7477.

Northern California Atlas & Gazetter ~ Published by Del Lorme Mapping Company: Great resource! Topographical maps covering all of Northern California from just south of San Francisco to the Oregon border.

Southern California Atlas & Gazetter ~ Published by Del Lorme Mapping Company: Topographical maps covering all of Southern California from just south of San Francisco to the Mexico border.

Camping

California Camping~By Tom Stienstra: Awesome resource! This book is a must for the California camper. Lists virtually every campground in California. I never go outdoors overnight without it. Priceless resource for planning your paddling explorations.

Camper's Companion~By Rick Greensan & Hal Kahn: This book is filled with lots of good advise on camping. You want to be prepared and comfortable when you camp out. This book will get you there.

Periodicals

Canoe & Kayak: A national publication that features paddling issues. They cover everything: regional and world-wide destinations, water-oriented enviromental issues, paddle gear, reviews of book and gear, quiet water, white water and sea water.

Paddler: Another national paddling publications. Also covers a wide range of paddling issues. Very informative and entertaining.

Sea Kayaker: Obviously, the focus here is on the paddling the ocean, but once you become a fanatic paddler, you'll want to get into it all.

California Natural History

California Coastal Access Guide ~ By Erin Caughman & Jo Ginsberg ~ This is a great guide to the natural beauty of the California coast, with an emphasis on conservation Lots of photos.

A Natural History of California ~ by Allan A. Schoenherr: This book covers everything about the natural world of California: basic ecology and geology, climate, rocks, plants and animals. Broken down into ecological regions, this book really does justice to the natural diversity of California.

Coastal Guide Books

California Coastal Resource Guide ~ By The California Coastal Commission ~ If you want to explore the California coast, this is your "must have" book. It covers the natural and social history of the coast with detailed listings for each water feature. One of the best things about this book is its use of photos and drawings to bring the coast alive. What flora and fauna live on this part of the coast? What has been man's effect on this arear? What a the geologic forces at work here? You'll find it in this book.

Exploring the North Coast~The California Coast From The Golden Gate Bridge To The Oregon Border by Jonathan Franks: This book is filled with lots of good advise on

Guide To Point Reyes National Seashore ~ By Dorothy Whitnah ~ Literially everything you ever wanted to know about Point Reyes National Seashore.

The California Coast ~ By ~ Donald Neuwirth & John Osborn ~ This book gives you lots of useful tourist information. The information is listed by County with sections on "Beaches & Attractions", "Lodging", and "Resturants". Exploring the food, art and accomodations on the coast is an adventure all its own.

Guide To Sea Kayaking Central & Northern California ~ By Roger Schumann & Jan Shriner ~ Before you just head off into the ocean you should be properly trained and equipped. Once you made the jump to sea kayaking (it's not quiet water) this book will give you some fabulous places to go.

Index of Waterways

Name	Page	Natural Waterway	Waterside Camping	Paddle-In Camping	Best Boat	Long Distance Paddling	No Motors/ Speed Limits	Exquisite Beauty
Abbotts Lagoon	61	x			Kayak		x	
Albion River	33	x	x		All		x	x
Anderson Marsh	42	x			All	x	x	x
Big River	32	x		x	All	x	x	x
Big Sur River	77	x	x		Kayak		x	x
Bodega Bay	55	x	x		Kayak			
Bolinas Lagoon	64	x			All		x	x
Carmel River	76	x			Kayak		x	x
Clear Lake	42	x	x		Kayak	x		
Drakes Estero	62	x			Kayak	x		x
East Park Reservoir	40		x		All	x		
Eel River Mouth	26	x			Kayak	x	x	x
Elk River	24	x			All		x	
Elkhorn Slough	74	x			Kayak	x	x	
Estero Americano	56	x			Kayak	x	x	x
Eureka Slough	23	x			All	x	x	
Freshwater Slough	23	x			All	x	x	
Gualala River	35	x	x		All		x	x
Highland Springs Reservoir	41				All		x	
Hookton Slough	25	x			All	x	x	
Humboldt Bay	20	x	x		Kayak	x		
Humboldt Lagoons	16	x	x	x	Kayak		x	x
Klamath River Mouth	14	x	x		Kayak	x		x
Lagunitas Creek	60	x			All	x	x	x
Lake Berryessa	46		x		All	x		
Lake Earl	13	x	x		All		x	x
Lake Mendocino	39		x	x	All			
Lake Merced	68	x			All		x	
Lake Pilsbury	38		x		All	x		x

Name	Page	Natural Waterway	Waterside Camping	Paddle-In Camping	Best Boat	Long Distance Paddling	No Motors/ Speed Limits	Exquisite Beauty
Lake Solano	48		x		All		x	
Lake Sonoma	44		x	x	All	x		
Lake Talawa	13	x	x		All		x	x
Limantour Estero	62	x			Kayak	x	x	x
Loch Lomond	70				All		x	x
Mad River	21	x			All	x	x	
Mad River Slough	22	x			All		x	x
Mattole River Mouth	27	x	x		Kayak		x	x
Navarro River	34	x	x		All	x	x	x
Noyo River	31	x			All	x	x	x
Pajaro River	72				Kayak		x	
Pescadero Marsh	69	x			All		x	x
Pinto Lake	71	x	x		All		x	
Russian River	52	x	x		All	x	x	x
Ryan Slough	23	x			All	x	x	
Salmon Creek	54	x			All		x	x
Salinas River	75	x			All	x	x	
Smith River Mouth	12	x	x		Kayak	x		x
Spring Lake	49		x		All		x	
Ten Mile River	30	x			Kayak		x	x
Tomales Bay	58	x	x	x	Kayak	x		x
Walker Creek	57	x			Kayak	x	x	x
Watsonville Slough	72	x			Kayak	x	x	x

The author doing what he likes best, upstream on the Albion Aiver.

John Coale was born in 1954 in San Francisco and has spent all of his life living and traveling in California. Since 1991 John has spent his spare time seeking out the canoeable waters of California. This book is the second of his books on quiet water paddling destinations, his first be *Paddling The California Highlands*. John has been a chimney sweep for 20 years. When John is not working or paddling, he's playing music on a plethora of different instruments. He's been a musician for 32 years. "Playing music and playing in nature is what sets my spirit free and heals my wounds."

Remember what Johnny sez:

"It's all right to have a good time!"

What are you still doing here? Go get your paddle wet!

Notes

Notes

Notes

Notes